Rotherham
Wellgate

'The Old Packhorse Route'

By Margaret Jackson

ISBN 9781905278535
Printed in 2012 by Pickards.org.uk

Printed and Published by
Pickards Design and Print Ltd, Sheffield
Telephone 0114 275 7222
www.pickards.or.uk

Dedicated to Ralph Jackson
1942-2018

With grateful thanks to John Jackson, Hannah O'Brien & Ron Bye

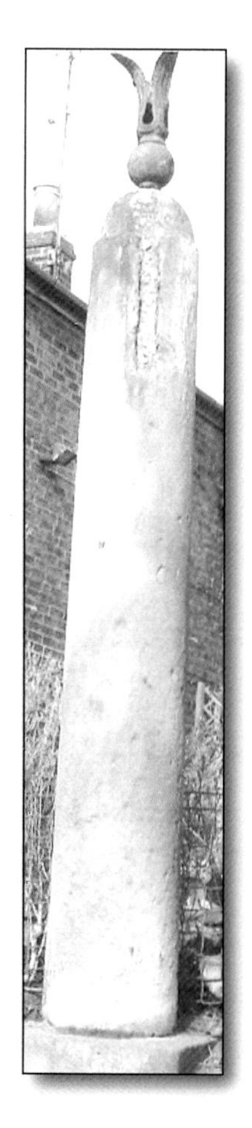

The last surviving oil lamp column in Rotherham Circa 1800

CONTENTS

Introduction

Wellgate can trace its history back to the will of Thomas Webster in 1490 when he left 3/4d 'to the making of a road called 'Welgate'. The main thoroughfare was part of the old packhorse route with coaching inns, stables and blacksmiths. Packhorses carrying all kinds of goods left town via Wellgate to Maltby and Tickhill on their journey to the ancient port of Bawtry. Travellers also left Rotherham via Wellgate and Hollowgate across 'the Broom Valley' to 'the Mile Oaks'and onwards through Whiston and Swallownest towards Nottingham, Northampton and London. In 1826 the road from Wellgate to the Brecks was turnpiked as part of the Rotherham and Barnby Moor Trust giving a direct route to Bawtry and beyond.

The 20th century gave way to new roads, trams and trolley buses moving towards the transport of today. Past and present merge with the hidden gems of Georgian style and Regency houses and the manorial site of Wellgate Hall and the Tythe Barn. Schools, Chapels, the Temperance Movement, Public Houses and the inevitable slums all played their part in the tapestry of the19th and 20th century.

We look at many of the surrounding roads and how they got their names as well as people of note who lived there. The wells and springs that gave Wellgate its name and how the domestic water we take for granted today came into being.

This book would not be complete without a nostalgic look at the shops which were household names, now gone, but not forgotten.

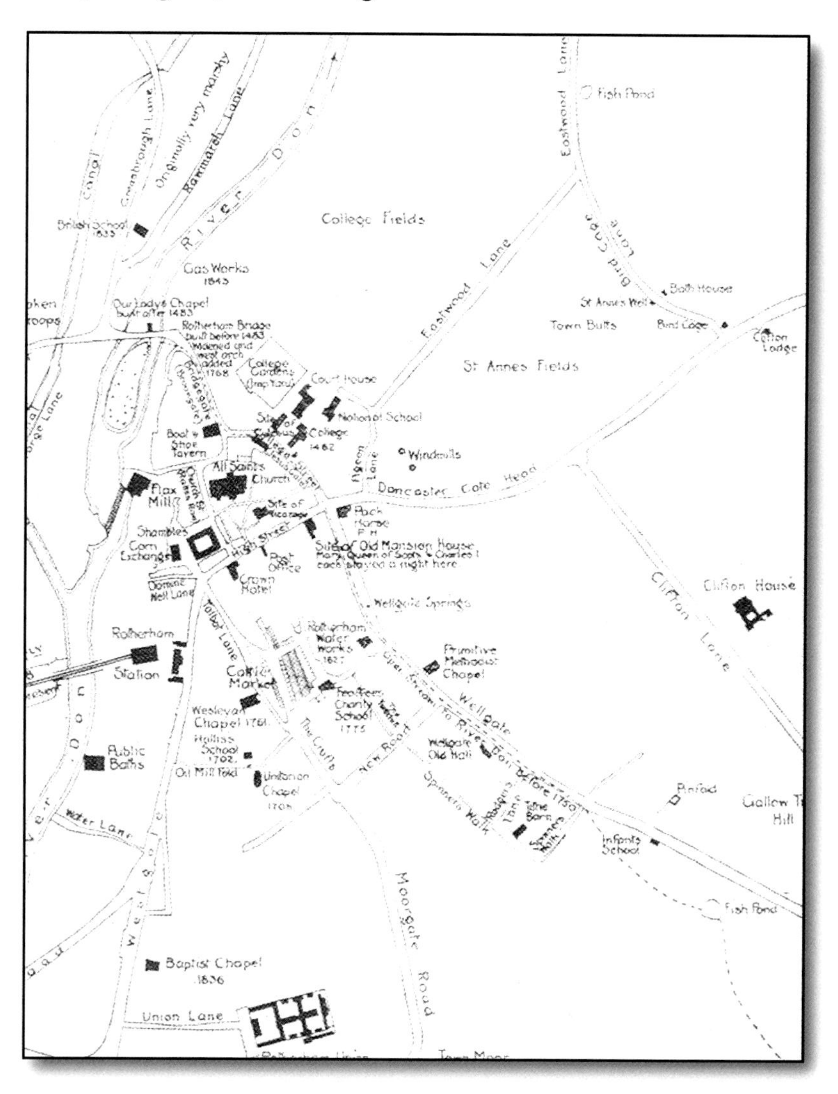

Wellgate was a main route into and out of the centre of Rotherham.

A 'way' or 'road' of wells.

Chapter 1

Wells and Springs

Wellgate was one of the main sources of water supply in the town and is named after the wells and springs found in the area.

Prior to 1827 the Feoffees are recorded as having responsibility for the town's water supply. 'Well' repairs are recorded in their accounts in 1569 amounting to £4 including 72 days work 'besides carting materials'. In 1708 nine labourers were paid 8/7d for 'cleansing Wellgate Brook'

Rotherham inhabitants relied on wells, springs and the Rivers Rother and Don for their water. There was no public supply distributed through the mains system and until 1750 the overflow from the wells ran down the centre of Wellgate, College Street, Bridgegate and into the River Don.

During 1750 the stream was covered over from the bottom of High Street. By 1791 water was carried above ground on the west side of Wellgate in an aqueduct which supplied spouts for public usage and also cattle troughs near the bottom of Vicarage Lane.

Ref 02180
Jesus Gate Well – College Street
Uncovered during extensions to Woolworths 1958

John Guest recorded that at a meeting of the Feoffees in 1790 'The Greaves consult proper persons what is the fittest to be done with the wells in Wellgate so as to accommodate both inhabitant and the street'.

After alterations were made, horses and carriages travelled in Wellgate 'upon a good level road whereas before they were wading through the brook often a foot deep in water, sand and mud'.

In 1827 a private company with capital of £2000 was established to provide Rotherham's first water supply using waters from the Wellgate spring. The water was pumped to reservoirs near Quarry Hill and the Crofts and distributed through metal pipes.

In 1853 this company was sold to the Rotherham and Kimberworth Local Board of Health who took over the public supply of water. By 1855 efforts to improve supply saw the completion of new pumping engines erected in College fields [Frederick Street] and service reservoirs at Boston Castle and Kimberworth using water from the Wellgate spring. These replaced the ones at Quarry Hill and The Crofts.

The Countess of Effingham regularly fetched or sent for a supply of the Wellgate water for her tea. 'When her ladyship drove into town, she invariably had two stone bottles filled with the water and placed in the carriage'

In 1851 an agent to the Sun Fire Office stated that 'not one in ten houses in Rotherham was insured. There was not much property that would be hazardous except some half - timbered buildings in High

Street, Westgate, Bridgegate and Wellgate and they paid double premiums'. Prior to the water works being established there were only private pumps and one or two public ones and the 'old cistern in Wellgate available for extinguishing fires'.

Wellgate Springs were the main water supply of the town and formed the greater part of the domestic supply until 1874 when the Ulley Reservoir was completed.

In 1890 the Rotherham Advertiser invited its readers to share reminiscences of the 1830's and 1840's:

Mr W Creswick wrote of water being pumped by an engine behind the Oddfellows Arms into a reservoir in the Crofts. He remembered Landlords fixing a tap in each yard and charging tenants a penny extra per week. Some tenants left their homes rather than pay. The water ran very slowly and there were a dozen buckets at a time waiting to be filled and sometimes fights broke out. On a Sunday morning as early as 5am up to fifty men with two buckets each were waiting at the Wellgate pump to carry water into Masbro'.

Pauline & Michael Bentley Collection   Wellgate Pump

Another reader recalled 'The grandest sight in our streets was a very large water barrel, drawn on wheels by a bull from Squire Fenton's at Car House. It travelled through Bridgegate and Jesus Gate to the Wellgate pump for water'.

The Wellgate spring water was abandoned in 1894 due to pollution caused by population growth and increased agricultural activity.

Inevitably the lack of proper drainage and the inadequate water supply caused many health issues. An inquiry by William Lee in 1851 highlighted the problems:

He found Roger Lane [Hollowgate] had no proper drainage and gave an example of three houses situated below road level which occasionally flooded, the floors were damp and had a privy under the bedroom and four 'piggeries' and another privy immediately behind. There was constant fever in the neighbourhood.

The privies on Mr Ward's property were above the roofs of two houses belonging to Mrs Holland and occupied by Scott and Pearson. The filth percolated under these cottages into Wellgate. The liquid from five 'piggeries' drained the same way.

Mr John Needham's property had two privies within 4ft 6ins of the houses and bedrooms looked into open cesspools. The tenants complained the stench was as strong in the bedrooms as in the privies themselves. Other examples given re iterated the above.

RFHS [JE Twible] Garden Row or Pass's Yard

Garden Row took its name from Garden Road. The name changed to Pass's Yard and by 1881 was known as Court 20. There was much overcrowding in the courts and Court 20 was demolished circa 1919.

The population of Rotherham had increased rapidly and the cottages in the courts and yards were overcrowded. There was no running water, outside privies were shared and the drains consisted of little more than a hole in the ground. Livestock kept in the yards added to the problems.

Mr Lee's conclusions were that although a water company was established in 1827 the quantity of water supplied was not sufficient. Health would be much improved by a constant supply of pure water in each house, proper drainage and cleansing and removal of decomposing animal and vegetable matter

Mr Lee recommended a charge per week for a cottage, to provide;

a] A constant supply of water with a tap in the house - one penny

b] Drainage of house, court and common privy with use of soil-pan apparatus
- one penny

c] Clean, durable and impervious pavement of courts and private premises
- one farthing.

d] Public cleansing of the courts and of the town by hose and jet - one halfpenny.

A report on sewage works in 1881 highlighted the flooding of basements in College Street and the east end of High Street caused by excess water passing into the sewer from the Broom Valley stream after being used at Aldred's Chemical Works. Problems arose in times of heavy rain causing 'much damage and inconvenience'. To remedy the problem a new surface water drain was proposed from the River Don to Wellgate below the chemical works.

Ref 11554 **Filling a Water Carrier in Wellgate 1910-1913**

In 1927 whilst working at the premises of John Simpson in Wellgate, workmen uncovered a 'beautifully constructed well'. It was thought that water had been sold from the well at one penny per pail.

During World War Two the rise in demand for water was such that Aldwarke and Wellgate spring water was used by the Power station for the production of electricity saving 200,000 gallons of drinking water per day.

In later years the supply was no longer needed for the power station and diverted into the river.

Cottages once stood on the site of 'Hartleys Tyres' and workmen uncovered a well still full of water, whilst excavating there in 1970.

In 1978 Yorkshire Water sealed the tunnel that carried the ancient spring in Wellgate for over 200 years. The tunnel, large enough for a man to walk inside was filled in to prevent collapse in future years.

The following formed part of a libretto of a pantomime performed in the theatre in Howard Street prior to 1898.

1] Of all the ancient British towns
Old Rotherham is most wealthy
Its just spent twenty thousand pounds
To make the water healthy.

2] And now the money is all spent
Pray is the water better?
Oh yes! It sparkles like the Trent
And could not be much wetter.

3] And all can have it who will pay
The Water Rate, but mind
That if they give a drop away
They're certain to be fined.

4] It is a sin to steal a pin
Much more the towns good water
As you may learn from Mr Slinn
When he collects next quarter.

In 1896 the Rotherham Advertiser reported that Corporation workmen were putting a new pump in Wellgate near where the old Wellgate pump was originally situated. Much speculation took place as to the reason for this; 'They've gotten't Sheffield watter now tha knows,' said one female gossip to another, 'An this'll be wheer it's bahn to be gi'en away'. 'Nowt o't sort woman', rejoined her neighbour. 'It's only a thing t' fill the new fire engine with'. More discussions took place once its purpose was known, that it would utilise the old Wellgate stream for the purpose of watering the streets. Conversation then turned to the goodness of the Wellgate water, its purity and 'tea making properties'.

Wells were to be found not only in and around Wellgate but also journeying out of town along Broom Road.

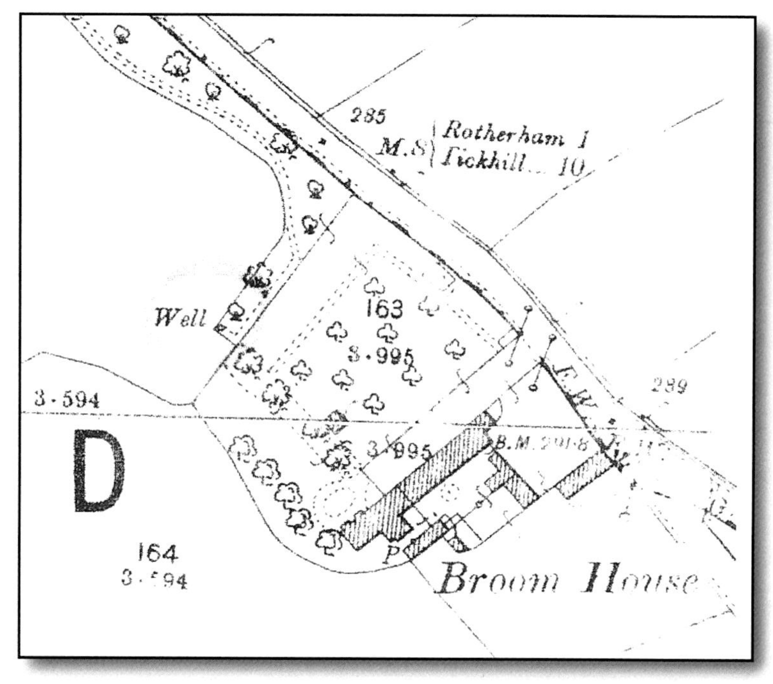

In June 2003 a well was discovered in a garden adjacent to the original Broom House, off Broom Road whilst renovations were taking place.

Shown on the 1888 ordnance survey, the well is a Shallow Dug Well built of dressed stone and approximately 46 feet deep.

In June 2005 restoration work began on the well. It had been filled in with topsoil and bricks and has now been excavated back to its original depth in the traditional way, by hand using a shovel.

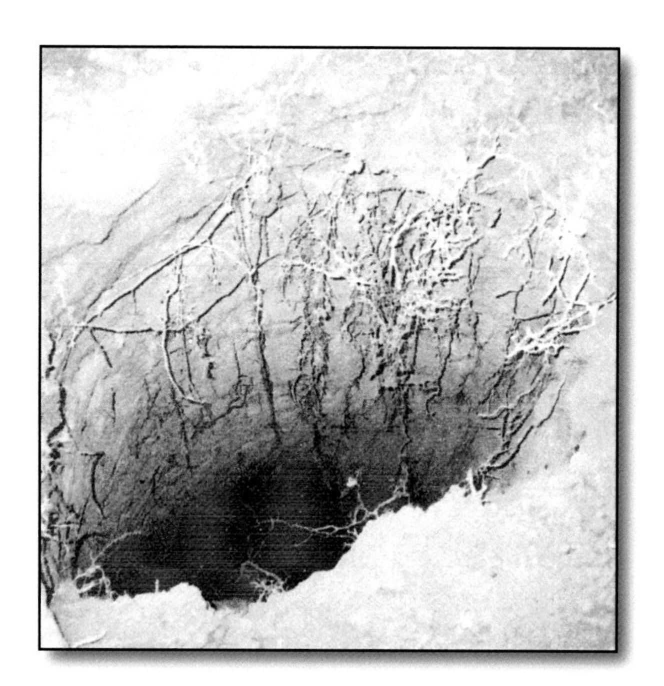

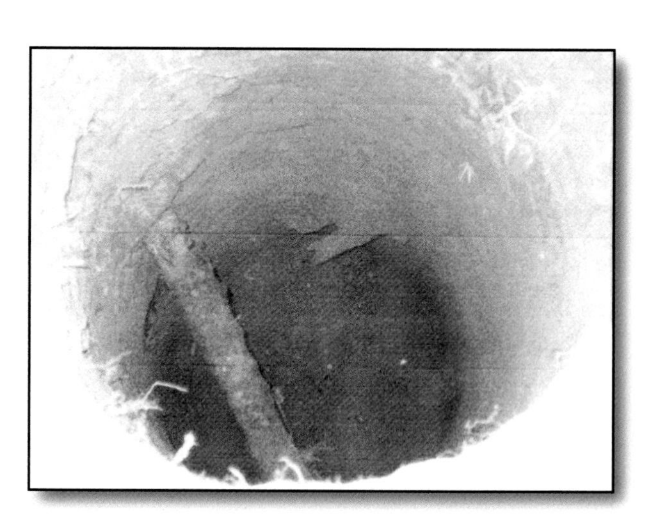

The well 'as found'

The walls of this type of well are often lined with stone, wood or concrete to prevent surface water entering the well and causing collapse.

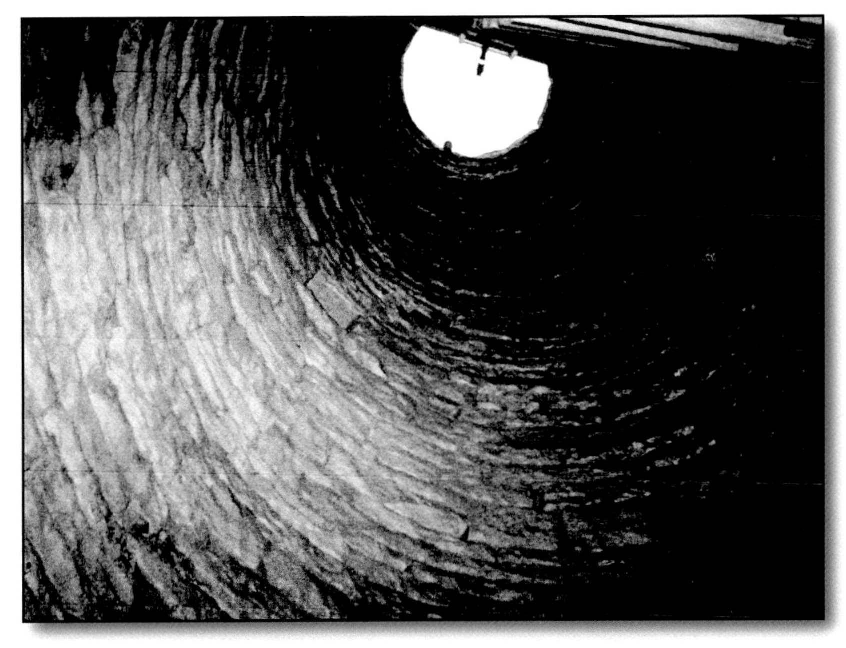

The well would have originally been built up to ground level with a wooden lid placed over the hole and served as a supply of drinking water to the surrounding area.

Completing work on the Well

The Wishing Well

Refs

Wellgate Introduction

Guest John Historic Notices of Rotherham 1879

Smith Howard A History of Rotherham's Roads & Transport 1992

Munford A P A History of Rotherham 2000

Rotherham Archives & Local Studies Service

Map: Early Rotherham, Drawing by Dorothy Greene 1925

Wells and Springs

Rotherham Corporation Waterworks

The History of Rotherham's Water Supplies 1971

Booklet The Feoffees of the Common Lands of Rotherham

Yorkshire Water Newspaper April 1978 edition 19

Information Mrs Barbara Littlewood

Munford Tony A History of Rotherham 2000

Rotherham Archives & Local Studies Service

Reminiscences of Rotherham & District Rotherham Advertiser 8/3/1890 Ref 942/741

Rotherham Advertiser 11/3/1890, 18/4/1890, 16/5/1896, 2/4/1927, 4/12/1970.

Guest John Historic Notices of Rotherham 1879

Guest John Rotherham Its People & Progress 1898 ref 942-741

Lee William Report to the General Board of Health 1851 ref 942-741/352.4

Mansergh James Report on Sewage 20/5/1881 ref 942-741/352.6

Ivanhoe Review June 1898 Volume 1 number 6 Price 1d

The Wishing Well

Information

Paul & Janette Haigh

Photographs

Pauline & Michael Bentley Collection

Wellgate Pump

Rotherham Archives & Local Study Service

Well Jesus College College Street 1957/8 ref 02180 Photographer Unknown

Water Carrier 1910-1913 ref 11554 Photographer Unknown

Rotherham Family History Society

Pass's Yard [Garden Row] Donated by JE Twible

1978 Wells loaned by Mrs Barbara Littlewood x 4

[Mr Tandy, Water Authority, Yorkshire Water, Mr Mosses, Rotherham Water Dept]

Paul & Janette Haigh

The Wishing Well from 'as found' to completion

1888 Ordnance Survey Map

Chapter 2

Schools and Chapels

Wellgate School

The Rotherham United District School Board was responsible for the building of several schools 1875-1902 including Wellgate. The school comprised 225 boys, 225 girls and 250 infants.

RFHS Wellgate Board School opened 2nd August 1879 for 700 children.

An H.M. Inspector visiting the school in 1883 remarked Wellgate was 'the first infant school he had seen without a boarded floor, to a delicate teacher or any but the hardiest girl or woman such a cold floor is deadly'. This was rectified immediately

Ref 13730 Wellgate School 1905-1910

Although the emphasis remained with the 'three R's' until the end of the century, other subjects were introduced. In 1892 the school held concerts towards the purchase of a piano for their music lessons. Geography, Science, French, History and Cookery were introduced by 1900.
The Inspectors report 21st March 1921 stated the school was 'staffed by earnest, competent and sympathetic teachers who had an excellent influence over a delightful, well mannered set of girls'.

Ref 00197 **Wellgate School Children 1921**

A holiday was declared 26th April 1923 on the occasion of the marriage of HRH The Duke of York and Elizabeth Bowes-Lyon.
A month later pupils listened to the 'address to the children' by the King & Queen through a Gramophone.

In August 1923 improvements were made to the large classroom when a partition of wood and glass replaced a woollen curtain.

Later that year Ruth Gilbody resigned as Headmistress of the Girls department and was replaced by Miss Edith Ollevant.

The custom of wearing a school cap bearing a school badge [W in amber] was introduced in August 1923. The children purchased them from George Miller, Outfitter, 2, Imperial buildings.
By 1925 Wellgate School had so many boys the headmaster created a new class known as Standard V1.

In August 1929 Class V were accommodated in the Meeting Room in Wellgate. The necessary furniture did not arrived in time and some lessons were taken outside and visits to Clifton Park Museum, the Parish Church and Boston Park were made.

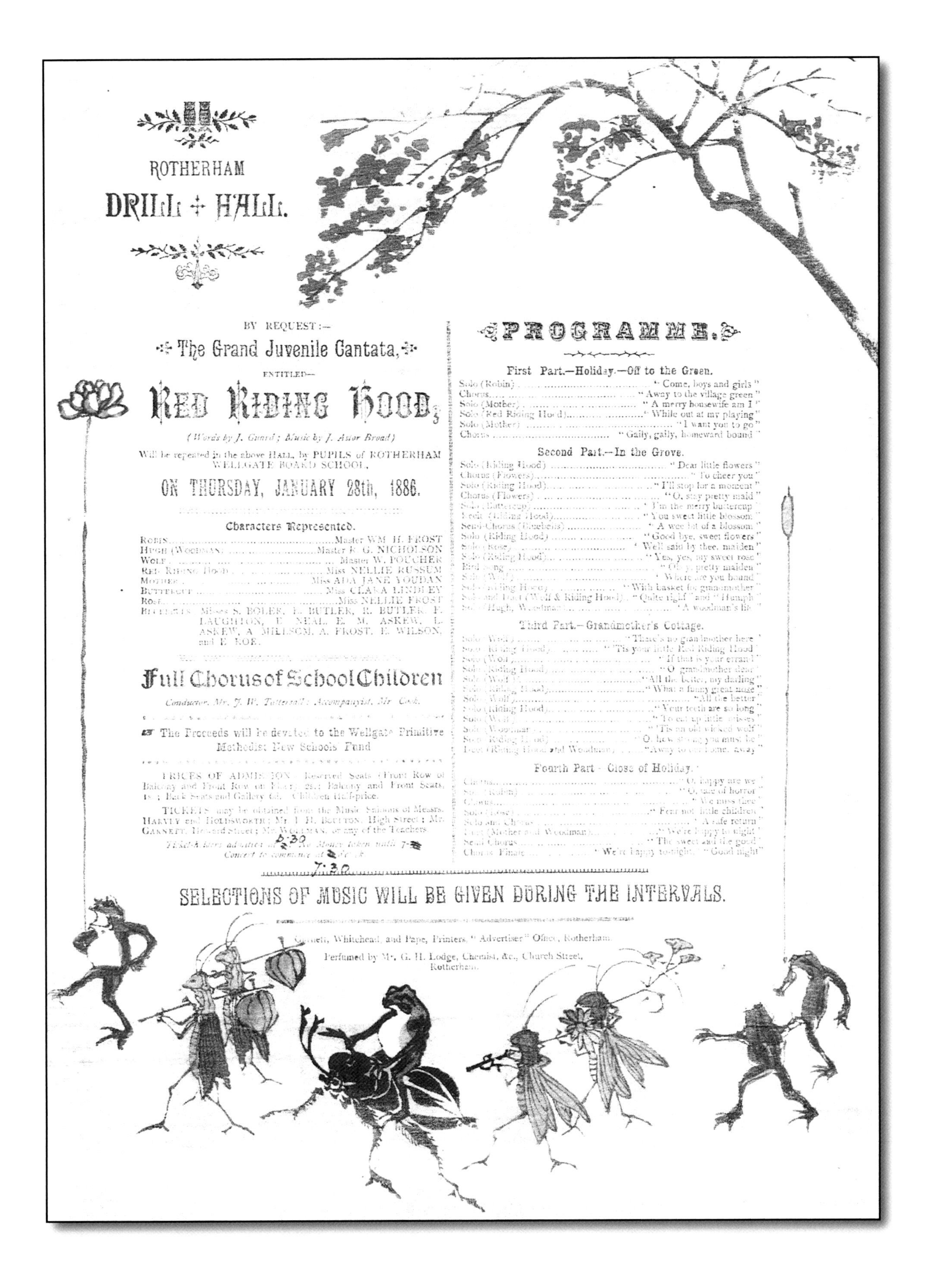

ROTHERHAM

DRILL ✢ HALL.

BY REQUEST:—

The Grand Juvenile Cantata,

ENTITLED—

RED RIDING HOOD,

(Words by J. Guard; Music by J. Astor Broad)

Will be repeated in the above HALL, by PUPILS of ROTHERHAM WELLGATE BOARD SCHOOL,

ON THURSDAY, JANUARY 28th, 1886.

Characters Represented.

Robin.................Master WM. H. FROST
Hugh (Woodman)................Master F. G. NICHOLSON
Wolf.................Master W. POUCHER
Red Riding Hood.................Miss NELLIE RUSSUM
Mother.................Miss ADA JANE YOUDAN
Buttercup.................Miss CLARA LINDLEY
Rose.................Miss NELLIE FROST
Bluebells: Misses S. BOLER, E. BUTLER, R. BUTLER, F. LAUGHTON, E. NEAL, E. M. ASKEW, L. ASKEW, A. MILLSOM, A. FROST, E. WILSON, and E. ROE.

Full Chorus of School Children

Conductor, Mr. J. W. Tattersall; Accompanyist, Mr. Cook.

The Proceeds will be devoted to the Wellgate Primitive Methodist New Schools Fund

PRICES OF ADMISSION.—Reserved Seats (Front Row of Balcony and Front Row on Floor), 2s.; Balcony and Front Seats, 1s.; Back Seats and Gallery 6d. Children Half-price.

TICKETS may be obtained from the Music Saloons of Messrs. Harvey and Holdsworth; Mr. J. H. Button, High Street; Mr. Garnett, Howard Street; Mr. Wollman, or any of the Teachers.

Ticket-holders admitted at 6-30. No Money taken until 7-[illegible]. Concert to commence at [illegible] o'clock. 7-30

PROGRAMME.

First Part.—Holiday.—Off to the Green.

Solo (Robin).................“Come, boys and girls”
Chorus.................“Away to the village green”
Solo (Mother).................“A merry housewife am I”
Solo (Red Riding Hood).................“While out at my playing”
Solo (Mother).................“I want you to go”
Chorus.................“Gaily, gaily, homeward bound”

Second Part.—In the Grove.

Solo (Riding Hood).................“Dear little flowers”
Chorus (Flowers).................“To cheer you”
Solo (Riding Hood).................“I'll stop for a moment”
Chorus (Flowers).................“O, stay pretty maid”
Solo (Buttercup).................“I'm the merry buttercup”
Recit. (Riding Hood).................“You sweet little blossom”
Semi-Chorus (Bluebells).................“A wee bit of a blossom”
Solo (Riding Hood).................“Good bye, sweet flowers”
Solo (Rose).................“Well said by thee, maiden”
Solo (Riding Hood).................“Yes, yes, my sweet rose”
Bird Song.................“Oh ye pretty maiden”
Solo (Wolf).................“Where are you bound”
Solo (Riding Hood).................“With basket for grandmother”
Solo and Duet (Wolf & Riding Hood).................“Quite right” and “Humph”
Solo (Hugh, Woodman).................“A woodman's life”

Third Part.—Grandmother's Cottage.

Solo (Wolf).................“There's no grandmother here”
Solo (Riding Hood).................“'Tis your little Red Riding Hood”
Solo (Wolf).................“If that is your errand”
Solo (Riding Hood).................“O grandmother dear”
Solo (Wolf).................“All the better, my darling”
Solo (Riding Hood).................“What a funny great nose”
Solo (Wolf).................“All the better”
Solo (Riding Hood).................“Your teeth are so long”
Solo (Wolf).................“To eat up little misses”
Solo (Woodman).................“'Tis an old wicked wolf”
Solo (Riding Hood).................“O, how strong you must be”
Duet (Riding Hood and Woodman).................“Away to our home, away”

Fourth Part.—Close of Holiday.

Chorus.................“O, happy are we”
Solo (Robin).................“O, tale of horror”
Chorus.................“We miss thee”
Solo (Rose).................“Fear not, little children”
Solo and Chorus.................“A safe return”
Duet (Mother and Woodman).................“We're happy to-night”
Semi Chorus.................“The sweet and the good”
Chorus Finale.................“We're happy to-night,” “Good night”

SELECTIONS OF MUSIC WILL BE GIVEN DURING THE INTERVALS.

Garnett, Whitehead, and Pape, Printers, “Advertiser” Office, Rotherham.

Perfumed by Mr. G. H. Lodge, Chemist, &c., Church Street, Rotherham.

Programme courtesy of Rotherham Archives & Local Studies Service

Performance given by the pupils of Wellgate Board School 28th January 1886.
Proceeds to the Wellgate Primitive Methodist New Schools Fund.

A 'free milk' scheme was introduced with eight children. Every child was seen with the intention of finding other under nourished children who should receive a supply of milk daily. By October that year another two children were added to the list for free milk.

Nora Grove was attached to Class 1 for teaching practice in Feb 1930 and this was completed by July 1930.

In September 1932 a 'New Milk Scheme' commenced whereby 52 children were to have one pennyworth of milk [one third of a pint] per day. In 1936 children receiving 'free milk' were weighed and measured by the school nurse and later examined by the Medical Officer of Health. From March 1937 both 'free' and 'paid' milk would be supplied by the Co-operative Stores.

At the beginning of September 1939 the school closed due to the 'international situation'. On 31st October home teaching commenced whereby all scholars were given the opportunity of being taught for one hour per day, ten homes and the school building were used. An air raid shelter for 300 was available from February 1940.

Irene Deville remembers the bike sheds in the playground were used as air raid shelters.

In 1944 there was a 'Salute to Soldier Week', a concert of plays and musical items given by the children to raise money. Collections were also made for 'aid to China' and 'aid to Russia'.

A new school year commenced in September 1951 following the transfer of a number of children to the new Broom Valley School. Departments at Wellgate merged becoming Junior, Mixed & Infants.

In February1952 a special assembly was held following the death of King George V1.

The following day children listened to the Proclamation of Queen Elizabeth 11 broadcast from London at 11am.

At Christmas 1953 Mr Hutchison in the role of Father Christmas distributed toys to the children in the infants department.

H. M. Inspectors visited Wellgate School in March 1956. There were 402 children on the roll comprising four infant and eight junior classes. Classrooms were said to be small and the building 'rambling and inconvenient'. The school assembly began the day with 'quiet reverence and the day proceeded without haste or fuss. The children were well mannered and at ease in their school, they worked well and with interest and were gaining much of value from their school life'.

In July 1958 the staff made a presentation to Miss Winifred M Beavis who retired after 43 years service at Wellgate School.

The high winds of 1962 caused much damage to the school and children were kept indoors because of the danger of falling slates.

In March 1963 children were given information about the proposed closure of the school at the end of the summer term.

Junior 3 class were able to transfer to their new schools, Alma Road, Badsley Moor Lane or Broom Valley after Easter.

In May the head teacher of South Grove visited Wellgate with a view to temporarily using it as an annexe to South Grove later in the year.

The 24th July 1963 saw the closure of Wellgate School. Children were dispersed to the schools mentioned above although a few pupils opted to go to Doncaster Road, St Anns and Herringthorpe.

The building was subsequently used as Education Offices followed by Amenities and Recreation.

Demolition in progress

In 1993 Wellgate School was demolished for housing.

Private schools were also to be found in and around Wellgate. In 1898 Mrs Emma Henderson had a ladies school at 'South Villa' Wellgate.

Between 1933 and 1936 Miss Sarah Jesse Henderson had a preparatory school for boys and girls in the schoolroom of Gerard Road Methodist Church

William Hartley and other pupils are seen here at Gerard Road with teacher Miss Wheatcroft.

Circa 1937-1944 the school became Rotherhill private school and the principal was Miss Ruth May Thompson.

Margaret Wilson nee Hartley is shown in the photographs taken outside the school at Gerard Road Methodist church and also appears below with her younger brother James Hartley. This school eventually moved into rooms in The Brentwood Hotel.

Early maps show an Infant school close to the site of the now Rotherham Evangelical Church and Whites Directory of 1864 records an Infant school being built in Wellgate by John Aldred.

John Guest attended a Dame school run by Mrs Spurr known as 'Dame' Spurr who lived in Wellgate.

Directories record a day school at 21 Clifton Terrace run by Misses Lydia and Mary Hannah Tildesley from 1881 until 1908. Margaret & Paul Findlater living in an adjacent house for thirty years from the 1970's tell of lead pencils often found when gardening.

Primitive Methodist Chapel

The Primitive Methodists began in this area with Camp Meetings. They were active in Greasbro' and Masbro' in 1819 and Rotherham in 1820. Services were probably held in the open air before moving into a room above 35-37 Westgate where church and Sunday school became established.

The Primitive Methodists transferred to a site in Wellgate in 1851 which provided a chapel, schoolroom and ministers house to accommodate their growing needs. The chapel, a plain stone building was erected by subscription.

There were seven trustees and the original cost of the building was £692 4s 2d.

By 1859 Rotherham was considered strong enough to be formed into a circuit.

In 1860 tenders were invited for the erection of a new pulpit and 'singing gallery'.

The original Primitive Methodist Chapel

The Pew Rents Book 1859-1870 show pew rents were charged according to where one sat, either the 'Bottom or Gallery'. In the chapel were 310 'lettable' sittings and 110 free sittings with approximately 350 people attending.

1870 'Bottom' records pews 1-36 at 1/3d per sitting and Gallery seats having different costs, pew 4 - 6d, pew 5 - 1/-, pew 13 - 8d, and pew 20 - 10d.

The chapel schedule reported that there were school premises at the 'end of the chapel' and in 1871 the 'Sabbeth School' had 33 teachers and 180 scholars

The chapel was the centre of 'vigorous and successful evangelism' and within a short time missions were established in other parts of Rotherham. In 1871 the Masbro' society was formed by missioners from Wellgate chapel. The first meeting was in a room known as the 'Shovel Shop' off Masbro' Street.

In 1892 four memorial stones were laid at the site of a new school to be erected on land adjacent to the chapel. The main entrance would be via Wellgate Mount and lead into a large assembly room. This was designed to hold four hundred people and be used for meetings etc including a schoolroom for sixty infants and classroom. The second floor comprised one large and nine smaller classrooms.

The New Primitive Methodist Church

In front of the schoolroom a new Chapel was built in 1893 [the original becoming the Temperance Hall]. Discussions were held in the Town Council because the building was situated forward of the building line of its neighbours either side. The votes of some members of the council known as 'Chapelites' supported members and friends of the new church and were responsible for allowing the church to be out of alignment with other buildings in the thoroughfare.

The new church was of 'Romanesque' style and held seven hundred people. It had an ornamental frontage with wrought iron gates leading into the church. From the outer vestibule hall staircases led to a circular gallery with elevated pews whilst downstairs the side pews radiated towards a rostrum.

The inside woodwork was pitched pine and the windows glazed with cathedral glass. Outside, the tower on top of the building was of 'considerable height'.

At the opening ceremony Rev Reynolds presented Mrs Woodhouse with a gold key to open the door of the church.

The chapel schedule 1894 stated there were 12 classrooms at the 'end of the chapel'.

The 'lettable' sittings were now 580 and free sittings 177.

Phyllis May Clarke and Jennie Maland appeared in concert at The Primitive Methodist Sunday School in 1917.

Double Wedding

Phyllis May Clarke and her sister Frances Irene Clarke were married in a double wedding ceremony to Mr James H Woolnough and Mr Joe Jones 28th February 1925 at the Primitive Methodist Church Wellgate.

They were the grand daughters of Alderman George Clarke JP

In October 1930 a committee formed to launch an effort to meet the special financial needs of the circuit. This was called the **'Twenty thousand shilling scheme'.**

The scheme would run for a period of three years. Members of the committee promised to show as much enthusiasm throughout the circuit as possible. The first event comprised a sermon, tea and rally. The charge for the tea was 6d and the choir asked to arrange musical items. 'Keymen' were appointed from the surrounding areas of Rotherham to promote events.

Fund raising continued in 1933 with a circuit bazaar held at Wellgate church over a period of two days commencing at 3pm each day. On the first day Wellgate was to provide teas and 'side shows', Eastwood chapel to be responsible for Father Christmas and Wickersley, the concert on the first night. The second day Parkgate were responsible for the teas, Eastwood the concert and 'side shows'. 'Soloists to be organised!' Approximately sixteen chapels provided stalls, sweets, cakes, second hand books, Christmas fayre etc.

‘A Bazaar is a temporary institution where visitors pay to enter, purchase liberally, and return home delighted that they have helped a good cause’.

Today a church bazaar would probably only last 3 - 4 hours!!

In November 1951 the Trustees of Wellgate Primitive Methodist church decided to close the premises for public worship and other activities and advertise the building for sale.

The Sunday school was being used by the WVS and the ‘Darby & Joan club’.

Members were consulted on their transfer into other Methodist churches. On the morning of the 6th January 1952 Rev C T Smith conducted the last service.

He also preached at Talbot Lane in the evening and said ‘We don’t want to stress this is a farewell - it is just a transference’.

Rotherham Corporation purchased the church and schoolroom buildings in December 1951 with the exception of the organ, communion rails and seating.

The organ was given to Tenter Street Methodist church and communion rails, tables and chairs to Dalton Brook Methodist church. Other furnishings were offered to Talbot Lane Methodist church.

Wellgate Primitive Methodist church was subsequently sold to the Freemasons.

Plymouth Brethren Meeting Room
Warwick Street South

The meeting room was originally a tailor’s workshop built in the garden of 49 Gerard Road. Kellys directories record it as a Plymouth Brethren church.

Prior to 1991 the building was used by the ‘Glanton Brethren’ It was then used as a meeting room for preaching and prayer meetings by the Brethren or Plymouth Brethren. Now closed.

Rotherham Evangelical Church

Rotherham Evangelical church traces its history back to an indenture dated 1886 when a piece of land in Wellgate comprising 272 sq yards was sold by William Easton to builder Mr Octavius Fox.

The indenture gives background information of an earlier document dated 1879 between [a] William Easton the owner of the land and [b] Rev Henry Partington and Rev John Thomas Foster Aldred the mortgagees.

By agreement with the mortgagees, in 1886 William Easton was able to sell a part of the land comprising 272 sq yds to Octavius Fox for the sum of £68 however the mortgagees retained an adjacent right of way for foot, horse and carriage in and over the piece of land measuring 4ft wide. A separate covenant between William Easton and Octavius Fox required the latter to erect and complete in 'good and substantial manner' fence walls not less than 4ft 6ins high with walls on the southerly and westerly side to be of stone but on Wellgate a small wall with palisades not less than 4ft 6ins high. 'No noxious, noisy, dangerous or offensive trade or business to be carried on'.

Rotherham Evangelical Church appears on the 1888 ordnance survey map as a Mission Room and the 1901 ordnance survey map as a Meeting Room.

It was the meeting place of a group of Christians known as Open Brethren. Some members previously belonged to the Brethren Assembly held in the Temperance Hall and others met at the Parish Hall, Moorgate.

By The Trust Deed dated 20th February 1924 made between John William Fox and Herbert Harry Fox [sons of the builder Octavius Fox] and six trustees of the church the property was purchased for £500. A mortgage was raised for the sum of £350, the remainder provided by church members. Rules were laid down stating the obligations of the Trustees in regard to the building, their duties, appointment and retirement.

In 1925 the meeting room was said to be 'quite dismal' with no floor covering, lit by side gas brackets and heated by a slow combustion stove situated in the middle of the room. By the 1930's alterations were made with a new kitchen, toilets, central heating and electricity installed.

The church has the facility for members to be baptised by immersion, the first being in 1928. Many such baptisms have since taken place.

The membership had declined in the 1930's and with little money available the Sunday school children were taken for their summer outing to Mr Archer's farm in Moorgate and Roche Abbey. Games and sports ensued with prizes of apples, oranges and sweets.

The first wedding took place in 1937 and the meeting room had to be registered for marriages with a registrar in attendance.

Membership which had declined due to the Second World War began to increase and a fund was established which resulted in extensions to the building in the 1960's including extra accommodation for the growing number of children attending.

The Meeting Room ceased to be a Brethren Assembly in 1985 and the name changed to Rotherham Evangelical Church.

Ebenezer Wesleyan Reform Church

Ebenezer Wesleyan Reform Church Clifton Terrace

The Ebenezer Wesleyan Reform Church moved to Clifton Terrace in 1970. Their previous home at Masbro' Wesleyan Reform Church was compulsorily purchased by the council for the building of the by pass at Centenary Way. The church building however was not demolished and became the home of Jemia Mosque.

In 2005 Dalton Wesleyan Reform church closed and joined with the Clifton Terrace Church. Now closed.

Gerard Road Methodist Church

Gerard Road Methodist Church situated on the corner of Gerard Road and Tooker Road opened in 1912 and replaced the Zion Church in Effingham Street.

The church traced its history back to 1850 when a group of Wesleyan Reformers met in a room at the bottom of the Parish church steps. In 1853 they moved into a room in Howard Street and then to the Zion Church in 1859.

The new site covered ¼ acre of ground and the foundation stones of the church were laid in 1911 by Rev TH Chapman on behalf of the Conference, Rev Foster Raine on behalf of the Church and Mr W Firth on behalf of the Trustees. Under the Trustee stone a bottle was laid containing a Rotherham Advertiser and Sheffield Independent, a preachers plan, list of trustees and a hymn sheet of the days proceedings.

The chairman spoke of the old Zion church built in 1859 as having fallen into disrepair and the congregation being 'incommoded on a Sunday evening by the noise and disturbance created by tram cars and crowds of people'. The Sunday school was of the 'cellar type' underneath the church and had no classrooms. The new church would be 'a very handsome building' with all the facilities required. Following the ceremony, friends proceeded to the Primitive Methodist Church for refreshments.

After disposing of the Zion church, members initially held services in Wellgate School before transferring to the schoolroom in Tooker Road whilst waiting for the church to be completed.

The church was designed by James Totty and built in red brick with Ancaster stone dressings. It accommodated 500 people with an adjoining schoolroom.

The organ was moved to Gerard Road from the Zion Church

On the 14th March 1912 Mrs J H Kershaw formally opened the new church. Sadly the minister Rev F. Raine who had worked so hard towards its completion died the following day.

In 1914 a concert was held at Gerard Road in support of the 'Belgian Relief Support Fund' attended by a number of Belgian refugees living in Thrybergh.

The Sunday school, founded in 1852 celebrated its centenary at Gerard Road in 1952.

Whitsuntide walks were a great feature of the 1950's with several churches taking part with floats depicting biblical scenes in procession from the old fairground on Main Street to Clifton Park.

In 1982 the 70th Anniversary of the church was held and former members were invited to join the celebrations.

Church members enjoying the 75th Anniversary tea

Five years later more celebrations took place at the 75th Anniversary when a silver key used in the opening ceremony of the church formed the centrepiece of the occasion.

A special service was held for members including visitors from other parts of the country and guests from Australia. This was followed by tea with a specially designed cake.

Three weeks later the church was broken into and the safe containing birth and marriage documents from the past 75 years were stolen. Fortunately copies of all documents were deposited with the Registrar General.

In 1997 Gerard Road and Clifton Methodist churches decided to amalgamate. The rising costs of maintaining Gerard Road and the proposed expansion of Clifton Methodist were factors in this decision. One hundred and fifty people attended a thanksgiving service. The church had been a source of friendship and fellowship for 85 years and the new congregation looked forward to planning and building a new church together.

Refs
Wellgate School
Rotherham Archives and Local Studies Service
Catalogue 62G-150-P
Kellys Directories 1881, 1930, 1948
1911 Rotherham Annual
Wellgate School Log Books 1921-1951 ref 77-E/41/5, 1951-1963 ref 77-E/41/11
Cater PM A Short History of Education in the County Borough of Rotherham 1871-1974
Beggs Thomas Sketch of the Life & Labours of Mr Alderman John Guest FSA 1881
Information-Bike Sheds-Mrs I Deville
Photographs
Rotherham Family History Society
Wellgate School
Rotherham Archives and Local Studies Service
Wellgate School 1905-1910 ref 13730 Photographer unknown
Wellgate Council School 1921 ref 00197 Photographer unknown
Wellgate Programme 1886
Philip H J Smedley, Rotherham Archaeological Society
Wellgate School Demolition [3]

Private Schools
Rotherham Archives & Local Studies Service
Whites Directories 1864 ref 942/74 SHE ST, 1898
Kellys Directories 1881-1908
Information Gerard Road Mrs Houghton, Mrs Wilson
Photographs loaned by
Mrs M Wilson

Clifton Terrace
Information Paul & Margaret Findlater

Primitive Methodist Church
Rotherham Archives & Local Studies Service
Guest John Historic Notices of Rotherham 1879 page 483
Methodists press cuttings - Book I & 2 ref 942.741/287
White Archive file 4 1-T to 44-RD 12/1, Pew Rental 1859-1870, 12/N 3/1-2 page 2
Rotherham Circuit Wellgate Historical Documents 1859-1903
Rotherham Advertiser 17th June 1920, 14/4/1860, 16/7/1892, 5/8/1893, 22/9/1951, 10/11/1951, 17/11/1951, 22/12/1951,
Wellgate PMC handwritten book 1930
Souvenir Grand Rainbow Bazaar 1913 ref 367-N/30/1/1
Morris E 'Eastwood View' ref 942 741/287
Rotherham Annual 1953
Pictures
Souvenir Grand Rainbow Bazaar 1913 ref 367-N/30/1/1

Photographs
Concert 1917 & Wedding 1925 Pauline & Michael Bentley Collection

Plymouth Brethren Church
Information K Marshall
Photograph R Jackson

Rotherham Evangelical Church
Information Ian Jones, Minister
History of Rotherham Evangelical Church
Letter from Mr Harold Brittain
Wellgate Meeting Room Rotherham Trust Deed 20th February 1924
Indenture 14th December 1886 [Transcribed by John Ridsdale]
Photograph R Jackson

Ebenezer Wesleyan Reform Church
Information EWR Church
Photographs R Jackson

Gerard Road Methodist Church
Rotherham Archives & Local Studies Service
Coward PB Press cuttings Vol 2 page l5, Vol 5 page 35
Rotherham Advertiser 8/7/1911 page 5, 16/3/1912 page 9, 5/3/1982 page 28,
20/3/1987 page 9, 10/4/1987page 3, 14/3/1997 page 10.

Photographs by kind permission of Mr Donald Hodgkinson
loaned by Mrs M Houghton
Whit Walk - Rotherham Advertiser

Chapter 3

Past and Present

Wellgate House

Samuel Moult 7th Minister of The Old Chapel, Downs Row 1743-1776 married Bridget Wylde in 1747. They eventually moved into Wellgate House described as having a 'spacious green frontage and broad drive with a large garden and orchard to the rear of the property'. The interior of the house had panelled walls, comfortable rooms and was referred to as a 'gentlemen's household'

Thomas Oliver Warwick, born 1771 became Minister of The Old Chapel, Downs Row 1793-1816. The congregation allowed him to study medicine at Edinburgh and London and in 1799 he obtained his MD degree becoming Dr Warwick. During his medical career he started the Rotherham Infirmary and was its first physician. Although returning to his Rotherham ministry Dr Warwick was also interested in chemical investigations and became known as an eminent chemist.

In 1796 **John Aldred,** grandson of Samuel Moult began dealing in Charcoal and went into partnership with his brother-in-law Dr Warwick in 1801.

The Chemical Works or 'Dye Works' was on a site adjacent to Wellgate House and produced acetates, wood acid, and textile dyes. The Turkey Red dye first introduced by Dr Warwick was a leading colour with the Manchester printers. The business was one of the first of its kind in the country but despite Dr Warwick's ability the business incurred losses. He retired from the concern and subsequently left Rotherham in 1816.

John Aldred continued in control of the chemical works and with perseverance redeemed the losses. He moved to live in Wellgate House in 1852 and died in 1856. After Aldreds death, Managers lived in Wellgate house and ran the Chemical works, of these William Easton eventually purchased the house and Chemical works from Aldreds Executors.

Towards the end of the century Charles Green occupied Wellgate House and used the garden as a builders yard. Around 1910 another building company WH Trehern took over the property and divided the house into three dwellings.

Twenty years later the 'garden'of Wellgate House was used by Moorhouse & Co Ltd, Taxi and Cab Proprietors, Wellgate.

Ref 00195 **Wellgate Garage 1939**

MODERN DAIMLER SALOON
MOTOR HEARSE
CAN BE SUPPLIED ON THE SHORTEST NOTICE
Telephone: Rotherham 69.
MOORHOUSE & CO.
(ROTHERHAM) LTD.,
The Funeral Furnishers.
COFFINS MADE ON THE PREMISES
Office and Garage:
WELLGATE GARAGE, ROTHERHAM

In the spring of 1964 Mr Les Nicholson bought the site from Moorhouse & Co consisting of Wellgate House and garden, the old sheds and the Esso service station in front of the house facing Wellgate.

Brittains furniture dealers used one of the sheds for storing their vans. Adjacent, a two storey wooden building was used by Moorhouse for their vehicles and then by Nicholsons for their cars. Upstairs was Smeatons bed company.

The land was bought from Mr Oxley who ran a funeral service and taxi business from the site.

The sheds were demolished in 1964 and the house circa 1970 to make way for a garage, workshop and showroom for Nicholson Bros.

Wellgate House shortly before demolition

Nicholsons was managed by Paul Nicholson until his father Les sold the land to Kwiksave supermarket in 1984/5. In these pictures the cars are absent having already transferred to their Maltby business in readiness for closure at Wellgate.

Wellgate Old Hall

The history of Wellgate Old Hall was traced back to the 14th century when a survey by Rotherham Archaeological Society in the 1970's found evidence of three phases of rebuilding, 15th, 16th and 17th century and a re-use of timbers ring-dated to 1479.

The hall was situated within an important manorial site bounded by Mansfield Road, Whybourne Terrace, Roger Lane [Hollowgate] and Wellgate. This included the Great Tythe Barn, demolished in the 1960's and a small timbered barn at the SW corner of the site, demolished during re-development by Kirby Central.

RFHS Colin Leonard Collection

In the mid 19th century Wellgate Old Hall was re roofed with Welsh slate and converted into four cottages. The first cottage from the left was occupied by Mike and Joan Ashworth in 1957 which they rented from Coopers the builders, Greasbro'. The cottage had a long front garden with a back yard and outside toilet. The entrance to the cottage was through the front door, there was no back door. The inside of the cottage consisted of a larder opposite the front door, a small kitchen and living room with a Range. Upstairs was one bedroom and a bathroom without a toilet. The cottages were eventually condemned and occupants re housed.

The hall fell into disrepair and was purchased by Kirby Central who wanted to develop the site. It was converted into offices over a two-year period in the 1970's.

Prior to re development an investigation by members of Rotherham Archaeological Society discovered two stone stacks of the 16th century were surmounted by limestone chimneys, and contained four fireplaces, two on the lower floor and two on the upper floor, one of which was in good condition and it was hoped would remain 'in situ'.

An arched fireplace with a keystone and stone baking ovens were found at ground level.

The 15th century framed wattle and daub building appeared to have been encased and roofed in 'Rotherham Red Sandstone' in the 17th century. Discovered on the site was a small Georgian teapot made of Leeds biscuit ware, a child's leather shoe, buttons and clay pipes.

Tudor Fireplace now stands in the forecourt of Wellgate Old Hall

Wellgate Old Hall was purchased by Cannon Lincoln in 1982 and used as an area office for the South Yorkshire and Humberside Regions. The building became the home of the Citizens Advice Bureau. Currently empty.

Wellgate Old Hall was listed as a building of historical and archaeological interest in 1951.

Hood Cross

A stone cross known as the Hood Cross was sited at the junction of Doncaster Gate, High Street, College Street and Wellgate and seems to have been a public meeting place. It was at the centre of 'some of the most respectable residences of the town'.

In 1595 Edward Redwarde and 'ye masons were paid 18/- for setting up of ye Cross' while John Pits was paid 3/8d for paving 22 yards at 'ye Hood Crosse'. The accounts for 1603 showed the high cost of repairs for the cross.

William Brokhouse and Ric Arnolde were paid 8/- in 1630 for getting stone and laying it at the bridge at the Hood Cross and making a new spout. Two years later Henry Radcliffe was paid 12d for cleansing the streets near the Hood Cross and in 1640 the Beadle was paid £4 wages for 'warding and cleansing the Hood Cross'.

Clifton Bank

Tucked away from the busy thoroughfare of Wellgate are the gems of Clifton Bank and Wellgate Terrace.

The 1851 ordnance survey map shows only an adjoining pair of houses known as 'Clifton Bank' at the head of the road facing towards Wellgate and two villas to the right hand side of the houses.

20-21 Clifton Bank

Early documents dating back to 1850 show the land had originally belonged to Rev. Jonathon Alderson [deceased] and contained 2 acres and 29 perches. The 1851 census shows the first occupant of 20 as Hugh Hoyland, Coal Merchant, and John Drabble Master Ironfounder at 21.

The 1888 ordnance survey map shows the road named Clifton Bank and the large pair of semis at the head now re-named 'Clifton Villas'. The two houses were joined by a central passage leading through to separate back yards.

In 1962 a dancing school, previously in the Crofts commenced at number 21 known as the 'Minnie Thompson School of Dancing', run by Minnie Thompson and Mary Leadbeater. In 1982/3 number 20 was also purchased and the two houses altered to form one property allowing for two rooms downstairs to form one large dance studio, a medium and small studio and dressing room. The adjacent houses 22 & 23 were also part of the school and used for boarding students who came from around the country.

An 1863 indenture mentions two stables and a carriage house built on the west side of the plot with right of way for horses, carts and carriages leading into Wellgate.

Clifton Bank, built in Victorian times mainly between the 1850's and early 1860's has many elegant Georgian style houses forming a terrace on the left hand side of the road. A series of arched passageways lead to the rear of the properties and low stone walls to the frontage add to the houses character. The properties have many original features including internal wooden shutters to the windows.

A detached house near the top of Clifton Bank built in the Regency style has been lovingly restored and contains many of the original features. Above the Victorian door is a stained glass fanlight. Two pairs of chimneys with arches were restored in 2010.

Below this house a sandstone quarry is shown on the 1851 map [this disappeared on the 1888 map] in the grounds of the large detached stone property, Carter Villa. Towards the bottom of Clifton Bank are the backs of the Regency houses of Wellgate Terrace.

Clifton Bank still retains some old cobbles within the road.

At the corner of Wellgate and Clifton Bank was the grocers shop of **James Jenkin**

RFHS The George Bentley Collection **79 Wellgate**

The 'Day book' 1898-1902 listed customers orders:
Tuesday 27th August 1902 Mrs Cawwood ordered –
1 Bag of Rolled Oats 10/-, 1 bag Bran 5/4d, 2 sacks 2/-, Total 17/4d
A reduction of 2/- was given for sacks returned.
Saturday 30th August 1902 Mr Henderson ordered 1 gallon of Vinegar 2/-.
30th September 1902 Mr Albiston of Boston Park had an order totalling £1-3-7 ½d
2nd October 1902 Mr P Henderson of South Villa ordered ¼ Spratts @2/6 = 7 ½d

James Jenkin was still there in 1912 but from 1922 - 1970 the shop traded as Beaumont & Stevenson.

81-81A Wellgate

The property to the right of the picture built by Joshua Walker in 1791 is listed in Samuel Walkers diary as 'a new house in Wellgate'.

In the late 1890's butcher John Chesterfield and watchmaker Irving Nash occupied these two properties. By 1908 the occupants were G E Cook, tobacconist and Richard Moody Butcher.

In addition to the retail shop Moody had a private slaughter - house in the yard behind the shop where he had a wholesale business.

George Humphrey remembered that the slaughtering began on a Monday afternoon continuing until 10pm.

His father R Humphrey had a butchers shop in Canklow and bought beef, lamb and pork for his shop which was delivered prompt at 7am on a Tuesday morning.

Deliveries were made by a motor vehicle with an open top cab and level wooden platform at the rear, without sides, back or top. The meat was covered by tarpaulin. The driver was Charles Outram who was a skilled slaughter man and worked most of his life for the Moody family. By the time Mr Moody died private slaughterhouses were shut down and animals were taken to the abattoir.

The rear of the building shows the Victorian extension

The advertisement for Moodys butchers shows a clock on the building now gone but the outline can still be seen on this modern picture.

In 1985 Philip H J Smedley won an award for the renovation of this building.

Wellgate Terrace

1 Wellgate Terrace was built during the Regency period in 1820. The house faces side ways on to Wellgate and in the garden is the last surviving oil lamp column in Rotherham circa 1800. Made of sandstone it originally supported a bracket and oil lamp providing street lighting prior to the introduction of gas lighting in 1833. The 'link boy' came with a barrow full of primed lamps and unhooked the used lamp and replaced it.

The lamps were taken down during the summer months and stored at 'Harry Lamplighters Stores' in Petty Coat Lane. By 1870 the cost of street lighting was £1000, an average of £2-12-6d for each of the 354 lamps then in use. In 1898 the number of lamps had risen to 1,200 maintained at a cost of £2688.

Grade 11 Listed

Wellgate Terrace, built during the regency period was known as' Dobbs Row' at one time after the builder.

Wellgate Terrace

The Temperance Hall

The Temperance Hall, Wellgate, and Caretakers house in Clifton Bank were purchased from the Primitive Methodist Chapel in 1895 at a cost of £800. Alterations were made to the building costing a further £400.

Mr George Eskholme, who had been connected with the Temperance Movement for over 50 year's opened the hall in January 1896. He was presented with a stirling silver key which was inscribed with his crest and monogram and 'Presented to G Eskholme Esq JP on the opening of The Temperance Hall Rotherham 25th January 1896'.

The Hall comprised a large hall, lower hall plus lecture room and three committee rooms. In 1911 the large hall was let for 12s.6d and the lower hall for 5/- per night.

Various societies used the hall. In 1911 a girls club from the House of Help for Girls met on Monday evenings and held a bible class on Sunday afternoons. The Rotherham Choral Society met for rehearsals and it was said 'The society was well conducted and deserved every encouragement'

Throughout the 1930's The Rotherham Amateur Repertory Company under its previous name of Rotherham Playgoers presented four or five plays per season at the Temperance Hall.

Plays by George Bernard Shaw and John Galsworthy, were regularly performed, often starring Jack Hancock. Agatha Christie and James Gregson plays also featured.

Two members of the company Cyril Bewley & Pat Bond wrote 'Rotherham Revived' and this was included in their 1938 programme. In 1940 the Society decided that due to the number of members on National Service and ARP duties it was impossible to continue their programme of now two plays at the Regent Theatre and three at the Temperance Hall. Instead they offered a programme of light entertainment consisting of one act plays, mimes, dances, songs and recitations whilst continuing with play readings.

After the war their name changed to The Rotherham Amateur Repertory Company and they performed in subsequent years at the Regent theatre and Assembly rooms.

In 1960 the Civic Theatre opened with a production of 'Pride and Prejudice' performed by the Rotherham Rep and the company moved there in 1961. They are the oldest dramatic society in the Metropolitan Borough having an unbroken programme of work since 1926.

The Temperance Hall is currently converted for shop use.

Workmans Coffee and Cocoa House

RFHS **[The building to the left is visible today]**

In conjunction with the local Temperance Movement Rev William Newton Vicar of All Saints Church established a workman's coffee and cocoa house in Wellgate. It was opened by the Mayor Mr J C Morgan on 9th November 1877 who congratulated the Vicar and thought the premises would be of great benefit to the town and in particular that locality.

There were concerns over the drinking habits of the townspeople and this was provided as an alternative. It was so successful that Rev Newton purchased the reversion of a lease for £1000 on a piece of land and a larger building with more facilities, St Georges Hall, was opened in 1878. The Wellgate premises continued until 1892 when they were demolished and the site used to build the Sheffield & Rotherham bank. Rev Newton was a popular person who used his private income for the welfare of the townspeople and gave a generous donation towards the Parish Church restoration in 1874.

St Georges Hall, Effingham Street 1928

The Masonic Hall

The Primitive Methodist Chapel 1893-1952 purchased in December 1951 by Rotherham Corporation was subsequently sold to the Freemasons.

Following the purchase of the Masonic Hall as it now became known, alterations were made to the building. These were completed early 1958 when a Dedication ceremony took place to mark the occasion.

The Masonic Hall is made up of four Lodges, Phoenix, Rotherwood, Fitzwilliam and Sandbeck.

The original lodge called Druidical Lodge was founded in 1773, consecrated in 1778 and met at The Red Lion public house.

The Phoenix Lodge existed in Rotherham from 1808-1830 and held meetings at The Crown Hotel, Moorgate Street, disappearing from the registers in 1838.

Records ceased until 1861 when a petition proposed by Britannia Lodge, Sheffield, granted a warrant by the Grand Lodge to Phoenix Lodge.

The first meetings were held at The Prince of Wales Hotel followed by The Ship Hotel and then in Domine Lane.

This latter building in some measure achieved the aim of the Masons to have a building they considered their own and was opened in 1888. By 1893 this building was sold and the Masons moved to St Georges Hall.

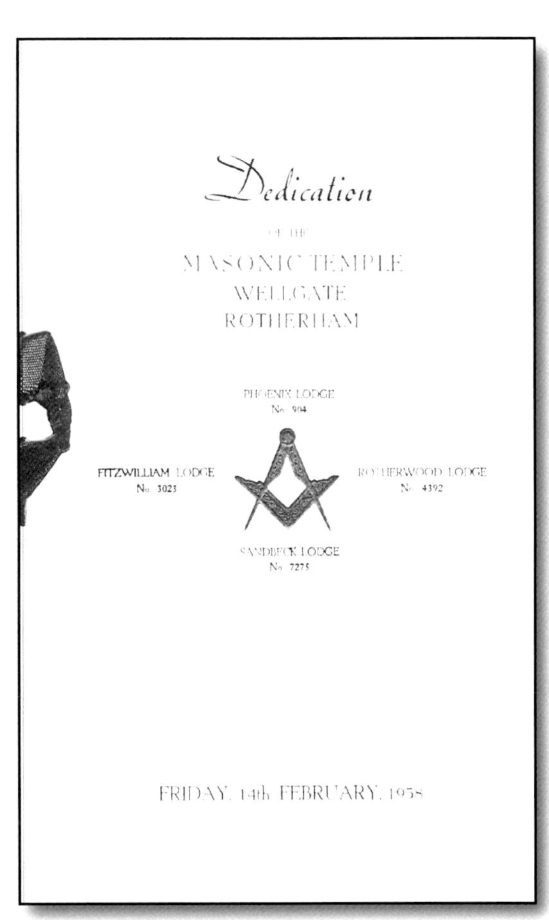

Dedication

OF THE

MASONIC TEMPLE
WELLGATE
ROTHERHAM

PHOENIX LODGE
No. 904

FITZWILLIAM LODGE
No. 3023

ROTHERWOOD LODGE
No. 4392

SANDBECK LODGE
No. 7275

FRIDAY, 14th FEBRUARY, 1958

The Masons played prominent roles in the laying of foundation stones and corner stones of hospitals and churches. In 1826 the Master of Phoenix Lodge assisted Lord Milton in laying the foundation stone of St Mary's Church Greasbro'.

They were involved in the laying of foundation stones for Dispensaries and hospital wards for the Doncaster Road Hospital.

Foundation Stone 1886

In 1886 the hospital was enlarged by the addition of a new ward and the foundation stone was laid on the 15th July together with a phial containing a programme of the proceedings, a report of the hospital, copy of the rules, plans of the whole building on tracing cloth, new coins of the current year and copies of the Rotherham Advertiser, Sheffield Telegraph and the Sheffield and Rotherham Independent.

Phial 1886

The ceremony was conducted by the Provincial Grand Master Thomas W Tew following a service at the Parish Church.

The Masons eventually moved to premises in High Street where a dedication service was held in 1898. The daughter lodge of Phoenix, Fitzwilliam, was consecrated in 1904 and held their Golden Jubilee in 1954. The second daughter lodge of Phoenix, Rotherwood, came into being in 1922 and celebrated its Silver Jubilee in 1947.

In 1953 Phoenix sponsored another lodge, Sandbeck, which bears the name of the estate of the Earl of Scarbro'. He gave permission for a part of his family coat of arms to be used as the lodge crest.

In March 1955 through the initiative and vision of past masters the Freemasons purchased their own property in Wellgate, The Masonic Hall, which gave them facilities for meetings, ceremonies and social functions.

Memories recalled in 1932 of an Earlier Time in Wellgate

[Most of these people appear in Kellys Directories 1883 & 1890]

A lady who wished to remain anonymous and lived all her life in Wellgate recalled the old plantation in the Broom area, with green fields extending to Broom Villas and the fish pond 'field' which was successfully fished [where Bartholomews Funeral Directors were situated until 2018].

Lower down Wellgate, the Plymouth Brethren 'fulfilling its essential purpose' and the Charcoal Works which extended from the cottages by the chapel to Wright's Paraffin shop, then a cottage.

Miss Easton's house, with its small plantation and the old spreading chestnut tree, under which 'Tom Booth, a man of enormous girth used to stand and advocate wider footpaths to walk on'.

Cottages, pig sties and stables were located on land occupied by Ball and Waite workshops and removal vans. Next to this were beautiful gardens extending to where Warwick Street is now situated.

Hollowgate had old Mrs Jennison and her little shop and after the Three Tuns Inn was Slawson's Yard and a blacksmith's shop occupied by Mr Dakin. Adjacent to Wellgate Old Hall was Radley Row and Mansfield Road was known as the Turnpike.

Mr Gate's baths are mentioned in Quarry Hill as well as The Rose and Crown hostelry. Harrop's little tobacco shop, Mr Bird the cobbler, Mr O'Neil's bakehouse, Mrs Hird's [famous for her pork pies], Laycock's boot shop, Councillor Joseph Wells the dyer, Mr Webster's rope shop, the old Mail Coach and Cleaver Inn.

On the opposite side of the road, The Pack Horse Inn and higher up Wellgate a rag shop, pawnbrokers and pastry shop. After Hanna Pass's yard was the Primitive Methodist chapel, or Ranters Chapel and beyond Wellgate Terrace, well kept gardens, Boomers Row and a blacksmith's yard with pig sties and gardens. 'Up' the yard was the entrance to Cookers field where the old Rotherham Town Football Club played.

Next was Mr Henderson's beautiful house with carriage drive and a large frontage [South Villa] known today as Sherwood House. Cottages occupied the site of the Masons Arms and adjoining shops, Tom Neal's sweet shop and Mr Turner's second hand clothes shop.

Whilst there was still a mix of business premises and dwelling houses the Wellgate of the early nineteen thirty's was becoming an important centre where every kind of shop and service were available. Some of the more familiar names even at that time were Richardsons newsagents, Dalkins Pharmacy, Heath's grocery and provisions, Edwin Clover, fish and game, Miss Pearson's gown and millinery business, Stephenson's Drapery store and David Price, Gentlemans Outfitters.

Refs
Wellgate House
Blazeby W Rev Rotherham Old Meeting House 1906
Guest John Historic Notices of Rotherham 1879
Munford A Victorian Rotherham 1989
Information
Paul Nicholson & Clare Watts
Rotherham Archives & Local Study Service
Kelly's Directory's 1902, 1910, 1930, 1970, 1974

Photographs
Rotherham Archives & Local Studies Service
Wellgate Garage Ref 00195 Photographer unknown

Wellgate House Rotherham Old Meeting House 1906
Dr Warwick Rotherham Old Meeting House 1906
Wellgate House at demolition Paul Nicholson
Nicholson Bros x 2 Paul Nicholson
Advertisement
Moorhouse & Co Rotherham Parish Church 937-1937 Brand Ethert

Wellgate Old Hall
Rotherham Archives & Local Studies Service
Listed Buildings Book 942-741/720
Bockley Agnes & Callear Veronica Wellgate Old Hall 942-741/720
Rotherham Annual 1953
Rotherham Star 30/4/1979

Information Joan Pybus Devon

Photographs
1] Cottages – Rotherham Family History Society Colin Leonard Collection
2&3] Dilapidated & current P H J Smedley
Tudor Fireplace Ralph Jackson

Hood Cross
Rotherham Archives & Local Studies Service
Guest John Historic Notices of Rotherham 1879
Clifton Bank
Rotherham Archives & Local Studies Service
1851 & 1888 Ordnance survey maps
Information
20/21 Mark Edgell
20/21 Mrs M Openshaw nee Leadbeater Mablethorpe
25 Clifton Bank P Thornborrow
M Jackson
Photographs
Old Clifton Bank loaned by D & J Clennell
Clifton Bank R & M Jackson
79, 81 & 81a Wellgate
Rotherham Archives & Local Studies Service
White Archive Catalogue 62G 150-P
James Jenkin 1/1Day Book 1898-1902
73/B Beaumont & Stevenson,
Kellys Directories 1898 & 1908

Information
P H J Smedley
D & J Clennell
G Humphrey

Photographs
Rotherham Family History Society
J Jenkin [George Bentley Collection]

81-81A Wellgate old copy David & John Clennell
Moody Butcher Advert P H J Smedley
81-81A Wellgate current & rear of building P H J Smedley
Rear Victorian extension M Jackson
Wellgate Terrace
Information
Rotherham Archives & Local Studies Service
Oil Lamp Listed Buildings Book 942-741/720
Reminiscences of Rotherham & District Rotherham Advertiser 1890 ref 942/741 1
Ivanhoe Review Vol 1
P H J Smedley

Photographs
P H J Smedley
R Jackson

Temperance Hall
Rotherham Annual 1911
Rotherham Archives & Local Studies Service
Rotherham Advertiser 1/2/1896,
Northfield Players/Rotherham Playgoers ref 512/G
Scrapbook containing press cuttings of plays & information by Donald Dale
Mr Stuart Lister Rotherham Amateur Repertory Company
Internet Information Rotherham Rep

Photographs
R Jackson

Workmans Coffee &Cocoa House
Gummer G Reminiscences of Rotherham 1927
Munford A P Victorian Rotherham 1989

Rotherham Advertiser 10/11/1877
Worrall J Moorgate Cemetery, A stroll around Victorian Rotherham

Photograph
Rotherham Family History Society
Picture
St Georges Hall 1928 C C Souter

The Masonic Hall
Information
C C Souter
A Bryan
Dedication Booklet C C Souter

Photograph R Jackson
Foundation Stone/Phiall M A Croft

Memories Recalled in 1932
Rotherham Archives & Local Studies Service
Rotherham Advertiser Extracts 19/11/1932
Advertisement Stephenson's
Rotherham Advertiser 25/3/1925

Chapter 4
Roads and Transport

In 1889 Mr Charles Green purchased the estate facing Wellgate from the executors of the late William Easton. Plans were made for the land between the rear of the Vicarage, Moorgate and Wellgate to be laid out in plots suitable for building purposes including five new streets. On this section a new street would be cut from Godstone Road together with two cross streets connected to Gerard Road.

1888

Another scheme meant Wellgate House would not be affected but the two fields belonging to Mr Hoare of London would be used for building purposes by running two more streets through from Godstone Road, one of which would connect with Hollowgate.

1901

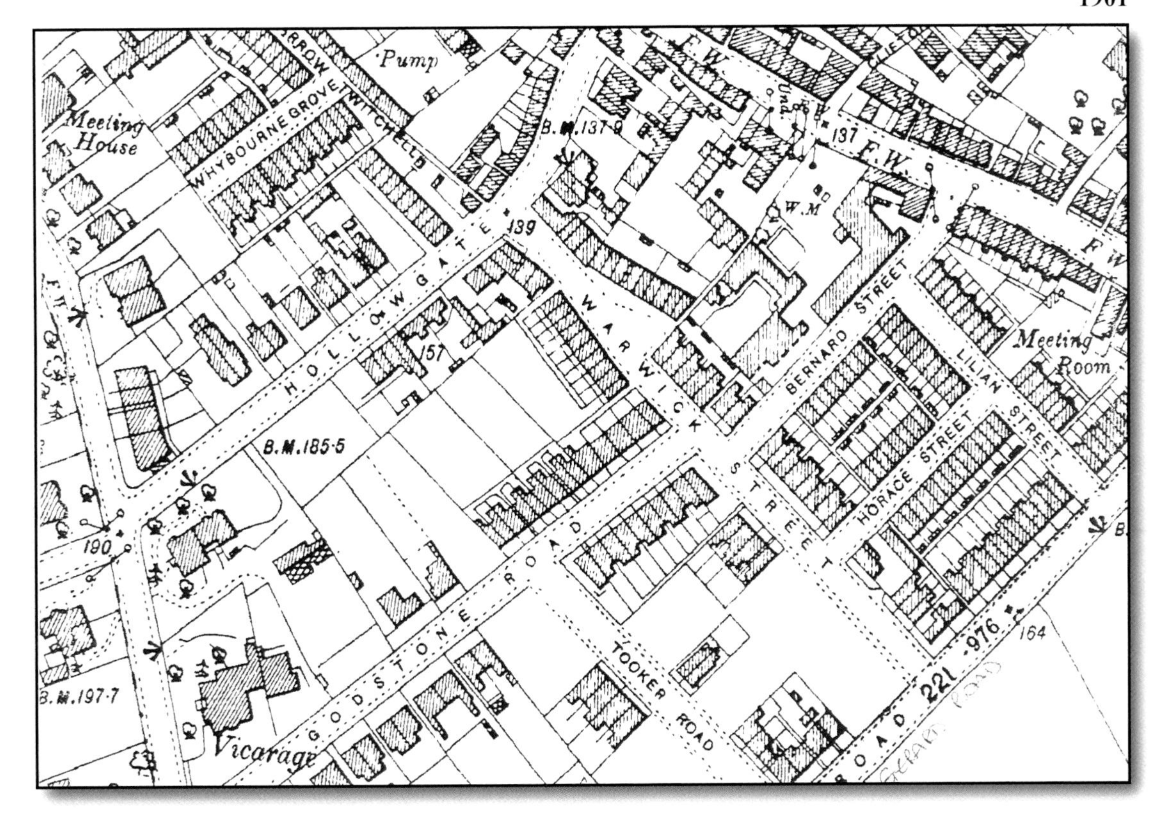

In 1834 a carriage called The Sun left The Pack Horse Inn at the corner of Doncaster Gate and Wellgate twice daily and travelled up High Street and Westgate and on to Sheffield. A few years later an Omnibus began operating each day from The Cleaver Inn to Retford and Blythe.

Mr Bletcher, Innkeeper of The Mail Coach was travelling home from Bramley by Omnibus when the horse bolted and he was thrown and injured. A few months later in January 1850 he held an auction on his premises and sold all his carriages, horses, harness, phaeton and Omnibus.

Ref 11553 **Wellgate 1904 -1907**

Carrier carts were allowed to stand in front of The Mail Coach and Cleaver Inns for the sale of garden produce and were joined by farmers' carts laden with fruit and vegetables on Friday nights providing a wholesale market in the street. Traffic became so congested that legal proceedings were taken and the market closed.

In the early 1900's Taylors bus ran from The Mail Coach Inn twice daily to Wickersley, Maltby and Tickhill and to Bawtry three days per week. In 1903 Wadsworth operated between Wickersley and Rotherham but by 1905 C Wright of Wickersley was providing this service.

Permission was sought under the Rotherham Corporation Act 1904 Tramways, to put forward a new tramway along Wellgate and Badsley Moor Lane to a terminus at Middle Lane. This was deferred in 1907 in order to seek permission to extend the line from Badsley Moor Lane to the junction of Wickersley Road and Broom Lane.

Roadworks in Wellgate in 1908 gave an opportunity to lay a single line of tramway to Mansfield Road. By 1909 it was decided to extend the line to a terminus at Boswell Street.

In 1910 Major Pringle from the Board of Trade inspected the Rotherham Corporation new Tramway extension from College Street to the Broom and the line of one mile opened. However, Broom residents objected to the charge of 1d fare and continued to walk leaving 'a grand procession of newly painted and beautiful looking cars' minus passengers.

By the cricket pavilion, Broom Road. Courtesy J Reader from Paul Fox Collection

Local charabanc owners provided services in direct competition to the Corporation. In 1919 Mrs May Clinton operated a Ford 'Motor Car' between Cleaver Inn Yard and Ravenfield.

A charabanc trip leaving Edwards Bros Motor Garage, 9 Horace Street

In 1923 Maltby residents objected to changing tramcars at the Broom and by 1924 the Trolly bus overhead wiring was extended along the tram route into Rotherham through Wellgate, College Square and Effingham St to a terminus in Howard St.

By 1928 street improvements were necessary in Wellgate due to increased traffic. Tradesmen were unhappy with the proposals and suggested it 'was an inopportune time to be spending large amounts of money' as they had experienced 'wretched times' over the past few years. The tradesmen agreed that improvements were necessary but were concerned at the extra cost that would be incurred in taxation.

Alderman G Gummer, Chairman of the Improvement and Property Committee was aware of the tradesmen's worries over the widening of Wellgate but sought to reassure them by saying that the scheme had been on the improvement agenda for thirty years.

EL Scrivens from Paul Fox Collection **Circa 1908-1924**

This picture illustrates the passing loop in the tram tracks and the electrical feeder to the right of the picture

As far back as 1900 the council had obtained powers to improve the part of Wellgate from the bottom of Hollowgate by the Three Tuns to Wellgate Terrace. Some cottages had been removed and the road widened opposite the Masons Arms.

Proposals included changes from the Oddfellows Arms to Hollowgate, the narrowest point being at The Temperance Hall where the road was only eighteen feet wide. A roadway of thirty-two feet wide or forty-eight feet between the buildings was suggested. The safety of pedestrians was at risk with the foopath being less than four feet wide in places.

The traffic increased considerably along Wellgate with the road carrying 1450 tons per day in 1915 increasing to 2000 tons in 1924 and 5000 tons per day in 1926.

The tradesmen were told that changes may not occur for up to five years giving time for compulsory purchase on some properties that would be required for street widening. However, it was thought that the longer the delay more cottages would be converted into shops which in turn would mean more compensation.

In 1928 the Chamber of Trade organised a meeting where the views of the shopkeepers were discussed. Mr Dalkin thought the improvements would be piecemeal rather than done at once so it would take many years to complete. The alterations were due to commence at Mr Dalkin's shop rather than the piece of waste ground higher up Wellgate.

Pauline & Michael Bentley Collection **Number 16 tram Wellgate 1929**

Mr Spearing expressed the view that the more the town was improved the more it would attract trade. He agreed with Mr Dalkin that there was congestion opposite the Primitive Methodist Church and if this were removed traffic would be able to flow freely. The trade vehicles were not the cause of congestion but the fault of the 'corporation vehicles'. 'If a dray were unloading outside a shop the tram had to wait or the dray had to move'.

Mr Dalkin said he had had to leave Bridgegate because of improvements and 'was going to be dealt with in the same fashion in Wellgate' Mr Spearing replied that the improvements suggested by Mr Dalkin should be put into effect and would serve Wellgate for a long time to come.

'Expensive shops could not be built for every trade but there could be more uniformity in the architecture, too late when the buildings are up'!

SLSmith. Paul Fox Collection **1928 Rotherham Trolley Bus No 52**

Mr Steel suggested there should be a terminus at Albion Road or Mansfield Road as customers were being taken directly into town affecting the Wellgate trade. Mr Cross expressed the view that the trams were the problem, he did not believe in trams, they were out of date, if, there were buses the traffic flow would be much easier

EL Scrivens Pauline & Michael Bentley Collection Early 1930's

[The Trolley bus in the distance is a Craven bodied Ransome & the car RHS an Austin 10]

Ref 00175 **Wellgate 1926-1935**

In 1938 Rotherham Corporation 'Improvement and Property Committee' recommended that the Town Clerk open negotiations for the purchase of properties from 42 Wellgate to Mansfield Road for the purpose of road widening. A re housing scheme would be put to the Ministry of Health for 'displaced persons of working class' to be re housed at Herringthorpe. These proposals would have included the demolition of the Hare and Hounds public house and were seemingly thwarted by the outbreak of World War 2.

Wellgate at the junction of Mansfield Road.

In 1945 Mr N Rylance, General Manger of Rotherham Corporation Transport Department issued the following notice:

'Withdrawl and Alteration of Stopping Places'

Inward Trolley Bus Stop - Bottom of Wellgate [near Thicketts Shop].

Outward Tram Stop - Bottom of High Street.

Owing to increased congestion at the junction of Wellgate and High Street and the dangerous practice of intending passengers attempting to board moving tramcars at this point it has been decided to withdraw the above mentioned stopping places after 7th February 1945.

This advertisement illustrates the electrical feeder box seen on an earlier picture. Although this has disappeared from Wellgate an example can still be seen in the Minster grounds, surviving from 1902 when the Minster first had electric lighting a few months prior to the first electric tram which operated from 1903.

In 1954 **KET 220** was delivered to Rotherham Corporation as part of a batch of 15 vehicles [215-229] intended as a replacement for the trolley buses and would run on the 'Maltby route' via Wellgate.

KET 220 was withdrawn from service in February 1971 and converted by apprentices and retired employees into an illuminated Christmas bus as part of the 1971 celebrations to commemorate the borough centenary. The bus continued to tour the streets of Rotherham at Christmastime until 1984. In September 1985 it failed its MOT and was left abandoned in a council yard.

In 1987 the present owner acquired the bus and restoration began in 1988. Eight years later the bus was back on the road in June 2006. The bus previously at the South Yorkshire Transport Museum, Aldwarke is now in Beamish Museum.

KET 220 Courtesy D Taylor South Yorkshire Transport Museum.

Rotherham Corporation Transport Department

NOTICE TO PASSENGERS.

The Corporation make every effort to maintain the services advertised in their guides or timetables but reserve the right to alter, suspend, or withdraw the running of any vehicle or service without notice.

The corporation will not accept liability for any loss, damage, injury, inconvenience or delay any passenger may sustain from any failure to maintain any of their transport services.

PASSENGERS
ENTERING OR LEAVING
THE BUS WHILST
IN MOTION DO SO
AT THEIR OWN RISK

Refs

Rotherham Archives & Local Studies Service
Rotherham Advertiser 16/11/1889, 5/3/1910, 7/1/1928, 21/1/1928, 6/09/1952.
Rotherham Express 16/7/1938
Hall CC Rotherham & District Transport Volumes 1, 2 & 3 1996, 1998, 1999
ref 942-741/388
1888 & 1901 Ordnance Survey Map

Information
Paul Fox
Jim Clark
David Taylor KET 220

Photographs
Rotherham Archive & Local Studies Service
Wellgate 1904-7 ref 11553 photographer unknown
Wellgate1926-1935 ref 00175 photographer AFS

Paul Fox Collection
The Trams up Wellgate Courtesy J Reader
Wellgate showing the passing loop system EL Scrivens Circa 1908-1924
Rotherham Trolley Bus No 52 1928 SL Smith

Charabanc Outing M Jackson

Pauline & Michael Bentley Collection
Number 16 Tram Wellgate postcard 1929
Looking towards town Wellgate Scrivens postcard Early 1930's

Philip H J Smedley
Wellgate at the junction of Mansfield Road

KET 220
R Jackson courtesy South Yorkshire Transport Museum

Advertisement courtesy Paul Fox
The Electric Railway & Tramway Journal Feb 10th 1922

Chapter 5

What's in a Name

RFHS George Bentley Collection Coxes Buildings

Wellgate was a main source of water from the several wells found there which supplied surrounding occupants and other inhabitants coming from as far away as Masbro' to the wells for water.

In the 19th century Wellgate was made up of several courts and yards, shops, trades, public houses, chapels and schools.

The courts and yards have now disappeared, Dobbs court, Walkers Yard, Aldreds Yard by the Chemical Works, Needhams Yard, Damcots Yard, Gillys Yard and Hoylands Yard.

Next to Appleby & Miles at 3 Wellgate, a passage led to Cox's Buildings and three terraced cottages. [chapter 6]

In 1901 surgeon William Collinson lived at 1 Cox's Buildings. In later years the Collinson family sold Cox's buildings and three shops on Wellgate for re development.

Churchwardens 1848

20/22 Wellgate is shown as part of the Charities belonging to the Churchwardens in a document compiled by the Clerk to the Churchwardens in 1930.

Under the heading 'Payments by Churchwardens and Feoffees' the two shops appear under 'Aldreds Dole'. The rents from these premises amounting to £95 were distributed with the Great Dole.

Doncaster Gate

Ref 6294 Doncaster Gate at the junction of Wellgate 1903-1906

The above picture depicts the busy shops on one side of the road and the Packhorse Inn opposite at the junction of Wellgate.

In 1806 a meeting of the Feoffees approved the establishment of a new Dispensary in the town and a house in Wellgate was let for this purpose at £10 per year. The Feoffees donated £20 and promised an annual subscription of £20.

The Rotherham Dispensary provided medical aid and advice in the treatment of accidents in Rotherham and Masbro'. When these premises became inadequate public subscription and a donation from the Feoffees contributed to a new building in College Square in 1828.

By 1867 a committee was formed to raise funds for a new hospital, Rotherham Hospital and Dispensary. The site chosen was a former cricket ground known as Babb's Croft, the joint property of the Earl of Effingham and Lord Howard. Fundraising fell short of the target set for purchase and the owners gave the difference of £678 as a donation.

On 19th January 1870 Earl De Grey laid the foundation stone and on 27th April 1872 James Yates JP opened the hospital.

The cost of the building plus 25 beds amounted to £9265. A further £1016 was raised by means of a Bazaar.

During the first 8 months the total inpatients reached 70 and by 1873, 120 inpatients and 1357 outpatients were treated. Expenditure had risen to £1314 and income £1241 with workmen raising £380.

By 1888 the surrounding population increased by 15,000 and it was necessary to enlarge the building. Another ward was added and named 'Central Ward' at a cost of £1204 which provided a further 20 beds, bringing the total to 45. Inpatient total had now reached 200 and outpatients 4569.

In 1895 further extensions were necessary and an appeal was launched for a children's ward. This was named 'Queens Ward' in celebration of Queen Victoria's Diamond Jubilee. It was opened in 1898 by Lord Scarborough who was presented with a silver gilt key decorated with the borough coat of arms surmounted by the crown and surrounded by a floral border.

There were 17 beds and cots and bedrooms for 5 nurses. The cost of £2545 was surpassed as fundraising reached £3986. The total beds had now increased to 62 and the hospital dealt with 366 inpatients and 5858 outpatients.

Increased demand necessitated the reconstruction of the operating theatre originally built in 1871.

In 1903 the hospital served a local population of 100,000 people. The accounts recorded a deficit of £1616 and Colonel Stoddart initiated an appeal to commemorate the Coronation of King Edward V11. The purpose of 'The Coronation Commemoration Fund' was not only to pay off the deficit but also to purchase 1200 yards of freehold land to provide more open space around the building. The sum of £2136 was raised which cleared the balance and left a surplus of £520 for proposed alterations.

The Nightingale ward for females was altered increasing the beds from 8 to 14. By 1903 the recorded number of patients treated since the opening of the hospital reached 140,000.

Dr Francis Charles Collinson 1872-1970 gave outstanding service to Rotherham and was made honorary surgeon at Rotherham Hospital, Doncaster Gate in 1904. He campaigned for over 30 years for a more adequate operating theatre and performed the first operation when it came into being.

Nurse Jane Peckitt [nee Gillan]

Above **Miss Alice J Buckle in charge of Queen Victoria Nurses**

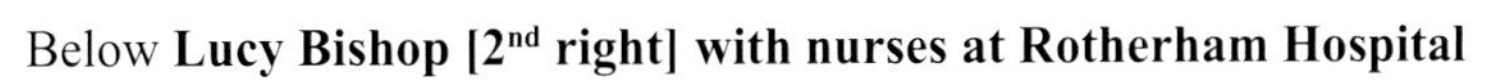

Below **Lucy Bishop [2nd right] with nurses at Rotherham Hospital**

1916

Nursing Staff with wounded soldiers at Rotherham Hospital during World War One 1916-1917

Lucy Bishop 3rd right

(Capital a/c)

Rotherham Hospital. **6141**

Dec 17th 1935

Received of Messrs Steel Peech & Tozer Ltd

the sum of Twenty one — Pounds

Shillings and — Pence being

a Donation to create Austin Torr, 41 Eldon Rd Rotherham a Life Governor

to the Funds of the above Hospital

£21 – 0 – 0 [illegible]

Secretary.

— In-Patient's Recommends issued.

2 Out do. do. do.

The above is a receipt for a donation of £21 received from Steel Peech & Tozer on behalf of Mr Austin Torr to the funds of The Hospital, Doncaster Gate in December 1935.

The donation made Mr Torr of 41 Eldon Road a Life Governor of the Rotherham Hospital. It was a position he was very proud of and gave him authority to visit the hospital at any time to check it was being run correctly and fulfilled the needs of the townspeople.

Hospitals and Infirmaries were maintained by voluntary donations and legacies. Governors and subscribers were allowed privileges according to the amount of donation. A life governor was entitled to two out patient recommendations annually.

In 1948 the voluntary system of management ended. On 5th July the Minister of Health took over the hospital which was well equipped, free of debts and had investments valued at £90,000. The Rev S B King presided at the last annual meeting of the Rotherham Hospital Governors and wished the new National Health Service much success.

The Rotherham Hospital and Dispensary 1872-1948 became Doncaster Gate Hospital.

Circa 1930

Consultant Mr Anderson in the operating theatre at Rotherham Hospital, Doncaster Gate, with Dr Sutherland in attendance administering ether. Note the nurse, not tall enough, standing on a box.

Mr Anderson was appointed honorary surgeon to the hospital in 1907 and retired in 1935.

High Street
The Royal Bank of Scotland

Grade 11 listed 1951 **2011**

The Old Bank founded in 1792 by Messrs Walkers, Eyre and Stanley was transferred to a joint stock company in 1836 known as the Sheffield and Rotherham Joint Stock Banking Company.

In 1890 plans were published for a new bank on the corner of Wellgate and High Street. Designed by architect Edmund Isle Hubbard, it was built of Huddersfield stone with Corinthian columns of polished red Aberdeen granite. The new bank opened in 1892 and the old bank demolished allowing a widening of High Street.

The first Rotherham manager Philip Hunt could be seen strolling down High Street every morning at eleven am. Dressed in a 'swallow-tail coat, silk stockings and buckled shoes with a pig-tail falling below his wig' he visited the Crown Hotel each day to gather information from the coaches arriving there.

In 1906 the bank amalgamated with Williams Deacons Bank Ltd who in turn merged with National Bank & Glyn Mills & Co, known as Williams & Glyn's Bank. In 1985 William & Glyn's Bank became the Royal Bank of Scotland and closed in November 2018.

Perhaps the most well known manager of the modern era was Mr Charles J Chislett. Born in 1904 and educated at Rotherham Grammar School he joined the Rotherham branch of William Deacons Bank in 1921. He became assistant manager in1954 and manager in 1955, retiring in 1964. Mr Chislett was a member of Masbro' Independent Chapel and became a Freeman of the Borough in 1967.

His leisure time was spent making cinema travelogues and short films. Showing these and giving lectures raised thousands of pounds for charitable causes.

Mr Chislett died in 1990.

Quarry Hill

Situated between Wellgate and The Crofts it was once the site of a working quarry. In 1827 a private company formed to provide Rotherham's first water supply using water pumped from the Wellgate Spring to reservoirs near Quarry Hill and The Crofts.

Three cottages 8,9 & 10 Quarry Hill were sold by auction in 1867 with an annual rent of £19.10.0d

Many changes had been made to The Crofts area since the mid 19th Century and in 1937 modernisation came to Quarry Hill in the form of a new Bakery built on the site of the old waterworks.

Ref 05611 **Vere & Sons Bakery 1937**

The high class Bakery of Vere & Sons was established on this site with the most up to date ovens, machinery and facilities together with hygiene and efficiency. They specialised in making bread and produced several different types in addition to the familiar brown and white loaves. Cakes and confectionery were also manufactured there.

The bakery had rooms on two floors with the preparation of bread, cakes and confectionery on the ground floor. On the upper floor confectionery and fancies were completed, packed and dispatched.

In 1975 the old established business of Vere & Sons Ltd was taken over by Hawley's Bakeries Ltd who announced expansion of the business at Eastwood and the ultimate closure of the Quarry Hill site.

Mansfield Road

Originally named New Road

RFHS Colin Leonard Collection **1964**

The Kimber family lived in the cottages numbered 2 & 4 Mansfield Road from the early 1900's until the 1960's and were listed as 'Ale & Porter Bottler' and then 'Mineral Water Manufacturer'.

Mrs Christiana Kimber is listed as early as 1881 at 75 Westgate Green as 'A Water Manufacturer'. The Kimbers business was adjacent to the cottages and they produced Mineral waters on site and distributed to outlets. Wholesale wines, spirits and cigarettes were sold from the premises.

The rescued petrol pump used by the delivery lorries in Kimbers yard can now be seen in The South Yorkshire Transport Museum, Aldwarke.

Examples of different soft drinks supplied by Kimbers

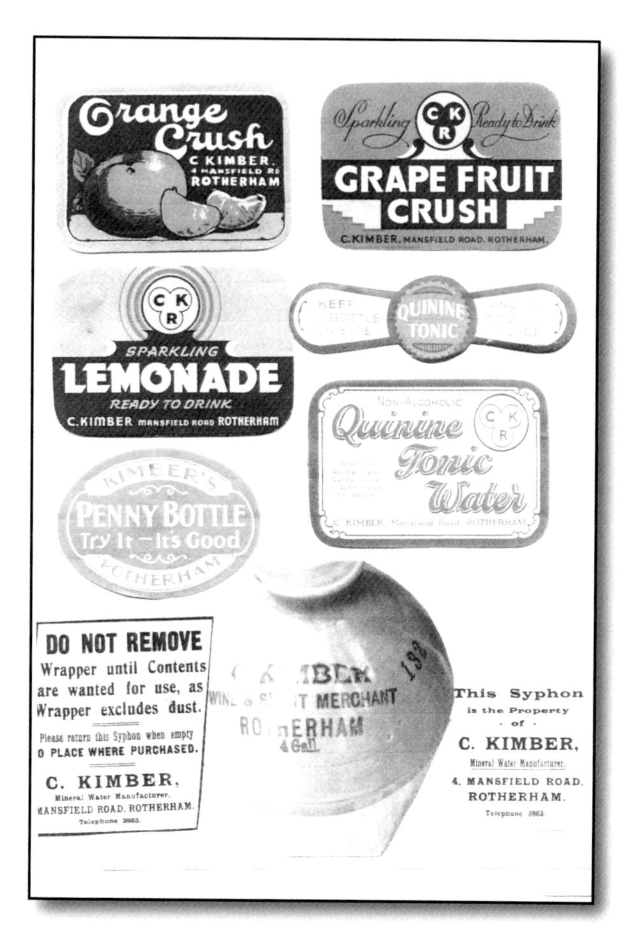

Mansfield Road, Kimbers, Hargreaves & the Barn

The plumbing business of Geo E Hargreaves originally situated in Tusmore Street moved to Mansfield Road in 1966. The business was established by William Ewart Hargreaves in 1921 and continued by his son George and then grandson John until 2005.

The Great Tythe Barn

Situated off Mansfield Road it was demolished in the 1960's. An informal survey by the Rotherham Archaeological Society discovered footings of a group of earlier buildings probably a Manorial establishment with brew house, tannery and animal slaughterhouse. [see Wellgate Old Hall].

The barn originally had an outside staircase leading up to a room at the top of the building. The outbuildings were used by Kimbers.

Demolition of the Barn

'Horse in Butchers Shop'

Whilst visiting friends in April 1904 Mrs Pugh of Rawmarsh left her pony and trap unattended for a few moments at the top of Mansfield Road. The pony, frightened by a cow in the vicinity bolted down Mansfield Road. It was unable to turn into Wellgate because of the speed it was travelling and the weight of the trap and ran across the road into the doorway of Mr Chesterfield's Butchers shop at 81 Wellgate. The shop was closed at the time and the shafts of the trap forced the locked door open and the pony through the door. The trap was badly damaged and the dazed horse suffered cuts. Fortunately no one was injured in the incident.

Looking up Mansfield Road towards Moorgate

In October 1912 The Rotherham Advertiser reported on a fire in Mansfield Road. The two storey building had a workshop on the upper floor and a coach house below containing a trap, harness and bicycle. These were destroyed and contents of the workshop damaged. It was feared that chemicals in the building might have been in contact with the flames and nearby occupants were evacuated. At one stage there was concern for the pony in the adjoining stable. It was thought the fire had started in the coach house below the workshop. Several men using buckets tried to put out the fire before the Fire Brigade arrived. Flames were seen in the shed even though the two large folding doors were closed. 'Someone with more zeal than discretion opened the doors and the fire spread to the upper floor'. The entrance to the yard was by means of a 'covered cartway' causing much difficulty for the Fire Brigade.

Albion Road [& William Street]

Joseph Stanley Crowther was born at 2 William Street on 30th May 1925. Eighteen months later the family moved to 30 Albion Road and at the age of five Stan commenced at Wellgate School. He came from a Methodist background and attended Talbot Lane Methodist Church.

Pauline & Michael Bentley Collection **Albion Road 1912, Houses on the right are yet to be built**

Towards the end of 1930 his father had to give up work due to illness and his parents converted their front room into a shop selling sweets, chocolates and cigarettes. Across the road on the corner of Mansfield Road Uncle George had a grocery shop known as Crowther's Stores, inherited from his father Joseph Crowther. [chapter 6 Wellgate shops].

At the time of transferring from Wellgate Infant School to the Boys Department the family moved to 8 Albion Road. Stan remembers watching the blacksmith at work in the forge in Wellgate on his way to school.

In 1936 Stan commenced at the Rotherham Grammar School and his family moved again to Godstone Road. After leaving school he transferred to the Technical College to take a one year commercial course. Stan started work as a reporter in 1941 for the Rotherham Advertiser followed by the Yorkshire Evening Post. At the age of twenty-six he decided to become a freelance journalist and spent the next twenty-five years reporting stories at both national and local level.

From 1943-1947 he served in the Royal Signals Regiment and was one of 4000 members of the British Task Force 'Operation Nestegg' sent to liberate Guernsey in 1945 after five years of enemy occupation.

To celebrate the fiftieth anniversary Stan was among 160 surviving veterans awarded a specially struck liberation medal.

In his leisure time Stan was interested in music and was a member of the Sundown Skifflers. As a singer songwriter and guitarist he co-founded the Taveners Folk Group who opened a club in the Masons Arms Wellgate in 1962.

In 1968 he was a founder member of the Rotherham Civic Society and chairman from 1992-2002.

Stan was a Rotherham councillor for 16 years and became an Alderman in 1967. He was a life member of the National Union of Journalists and held the silver medal of the TGWU. In appreciation of his service to the steel industry he was presented with the Iron & Steel Trades Confederation Shield.

He was elected Mayor of Rotherham in 1971-1972 and 1975-1976 and became Member of Parliament for Rotherham 1976-1992.

Hollowgate

Originally known as Roger Lane it was part of the old packhorse route for travellers journeying into and out of Rotherham via Wellgate.

A row of unoccupied dwellings on the west side of Hollowgate 1937 **Ref 08667**

Thomas Pillsworth, Blacksmith, is recorded as being at 2 Hollowgate from 1916 to 1925. Blacksmiths were also to be found in Wellgate and Vicarage Lane.

In March 1859 Articles of agreement were drawn up between Thomas Ironmonger the Elder, Thomas Ironmonger his son and Samuel Whittington, Blacksmith.

The agreement placed son Thomas Ironmonger with the Blacksmith for a period of two years to learn the trade. He would be a hired workman or servant and faithfully to the best of his ability perform such duties and keep all secrets relating to that trade.

The employer for his part would find full employment and teach and instruct in the trade of Blacksmith. He would also provide sufficient food, drink and lodgings during the two years. Weekly wages of three shillings for the first year and four and sixpence for the second year to be paid for every full weeks work completed.

In May 1859 Samuel Whittington and his sons entered into a partnership in the business of Blacksmith. The trade was carried on in premises in Wellgate and College Street. The agreement included 'Stock in trade working tools and 'things now, in and upon and about the said shops'. The business was valued by Robert Awdas a Sheffield Blacksmith and amounted to £93.9s.4d.

By 1881 Samuel Whittington was recorded as being at Norfolk Street.

Vicarage Lane to Wellgate

In 1802 George **Adams** was bound as an apprentice to his mother who had taken over the **Blacksmith** business after the death of her husband Thomas. George was joined by his brother Henry (1791-1864) who continued as a blacksmith the death of George in1836.

Ref 10297 Percy Harry Stuart Willie

The Smithy is recorded in Vicarage Lane from the early 1800's. Henry Adams [1856-1898] continued the business as Blacksmith and his son Henry is shown on the 1911 census as a shoeing smith. Gentry visited Vicarage Lane from miles around to have their horses re-shod by the Adams brothers.

The above picture shows the brothers outside the Vicarage Lane Smithy in 1931 before it was demolished for improvements to College Street. An Advertiser reporter visiting at that time to bid farewell to the premises stated 'the sparks were still flying from the anvil in this popular rendezvous for children and village gossip'.

After demolition the brothers re-located to 115 Wellgate in the early 1930's. The main business had been shoeing horses but in later years included work with agricultural implements. By the 1950's Stuart Adams was the last Blacksmith, his three brothers in the trade having died. Mr Tom Pashley of Wickersley recalled that the Adams brothers had shod for three generations of his family. As the last customer he was allowed to shoe his own horse closely watched by the Blacksmith. Stuart 'Stu' Adams died in 1958.

The house of Adams the Blacksmith next to the forge in Wellgate during demolition

Sherwood Crescent

Sherwood House situated at the top of Sherwood Crescent was formally known as 'South Villa' and is shown on the 1890 ordnance survey at the head of a tree lined road.

The 1851 & 1861 census records George Haywood Iron Founder and his family as living there. Born in 1805 Haywood initially worked in Sheffield before he returned to Rotherham to work at the Phoenix foundry, Masbro' of Messrs Sandford & Yates. After the dissolution of this business he joined Yates as Stove Grate Manufacturers at the Butter Market foundry. These premises proved to be too small and another business opened at the Effingham Works where John Drabble joined them as a partner.

In the 1850's larger new premises were built in front of the old works retaining the name 'Effingham Works'.Yates and Haywood were regarded as the founders of the stove grate industry in the area. John Drabble stayed until ill health forced his retirement in 1868.

In 1841 both James Yates & George Haywood lost a son in the Masbro, boat disaster.

After the retirement of James Yates in 1874, George Haywood became the head of the company. In 1879 he also retired. Among other interests, he was Director of Parkgate Iron Co & North Central Wagon Co, member of the Board of Health, Chairman of Rotherham Gas Light & Coke Co, Feoffee and Greave of the Common Lands of Rotherham and he also contributed to many charities. Haywood was a teacher and superintendant at Masbro' Independent Chapel and as Chairman of the committee laid the foundation stone at the new Doncaster Road Congregational Church in May 1866, standing in for Mr Mark Firth who was unable to be at the ceremony. John Mason, Jeweller, presented him with a mallet & silver trowel to mark the occasion. A bottle containing a parchment document was placed in a cavity by the foundation stone. George Haywood moved to live at Rotherstoke, Moorgate where he died in 1883.

The 1881, 1891, & 1901 census show occupants of South Villa were the Henderson family.

The original 1960's signage

Situated between Hollowgate and Whybourne Terrace

'A narrow path or passage between two walls or hedges'

RFHS Colin Leonard 1964

Spinners Walk

In the 1930's the narrow footpath between Court 13 and Moorhouses Garage connected Wellgate to Hollowgate and was known as Spinners Walk.

The footpath is still there today between the Pak Supermarket and the petrol station and leads to Warwick Street.

RFHS Colin Leonard 1965

Pinfold Lane

The Pinfold, situated in Pinfold Lane was a pen where stray animals were kept safe until their owners collected them upon payment of a fine. The Feoffees paid the 'Pinder' for mending the Pinfold Gate. Originally a wooden Pinfold, it was rebuilt in stone in 1643.

A schedule, listing Hollis Trust documents 1775 mentions a conveyance of land in Pinfold Hill [afterwards called Wellgate near Rotherham].

Albany Street

Bailey Bridge over the River Don at Eastwood

Donald Coleman Bailey was born in 1901 at 24 Albany Street. Within two years the family moved and by 1906 were living in Broom Road. Bailey was educated at Rotherham Grammar School and the Leys School Cambridge and graduated from Sheffield University in 1923. He was employed by Rowntree of York, the Civil Engineers Department LMSR and City Engineers Department, Sheffield.

In 1928 Bailey joined the War Office as a Civil Engineering designer at the Experimental Bridging Establishment, Christchurch. In 1936 he began to formulate the idea of a transportable bridge, bolted together, able to be carried by six men and moved by lorry.

Bailey was given the go ahead in 1941 to design an all purpose bridge which became known as the Bailey Bridge. Over 2000 of these bridges were erected during 1944-45 in North West Europe, Italy and the Far East. The bridge played a crucial role during World War 11.

In 1944 Bailey received the OBE followed by a knighthood in 1946.

The Rotherham Bailey Bridge was originally built in 1947 and rebuilt and re-dedicated in 1992.

Sir Donald Coleman Bailey died in 1985.

A child of the late 1920's in Albany Street

Warwick Street **Thomas Oliver Warwick 1771-1852**

Dr Warwick became the tenth minister of The Old Chapel, Downs Row 1793-1816.

He was the son of Rev Thomas Warwick a Methodist minister. In November 1800 he married Mary Aldred, daughter of Rev Ebenezer Aldred. Dr Warwick was very well thought of, the kind of person who would make a friend for life and advise and assist where necessary. It was said he was a philanthropic man who worked to do all the good he could to every man, woman and child he encountered.

[information about Dr Warwick can be found in Chapter 3 Wellgate House]

Aldred Street **John Aldred Died September 1856**

John Aldred was connected with the Old Chapel, Downs Row at the time when Dr Warwick became minister in 1793. Under a deed dated June 1813 he was appointed trustee of the chapel and his name appears in a list of seat holders paying £5.5s.0d per year in 1815. He joined in partnership with Dr Warwick in the chemical works in Wellgate in 1801, eventually moving to live at Wellgate House.

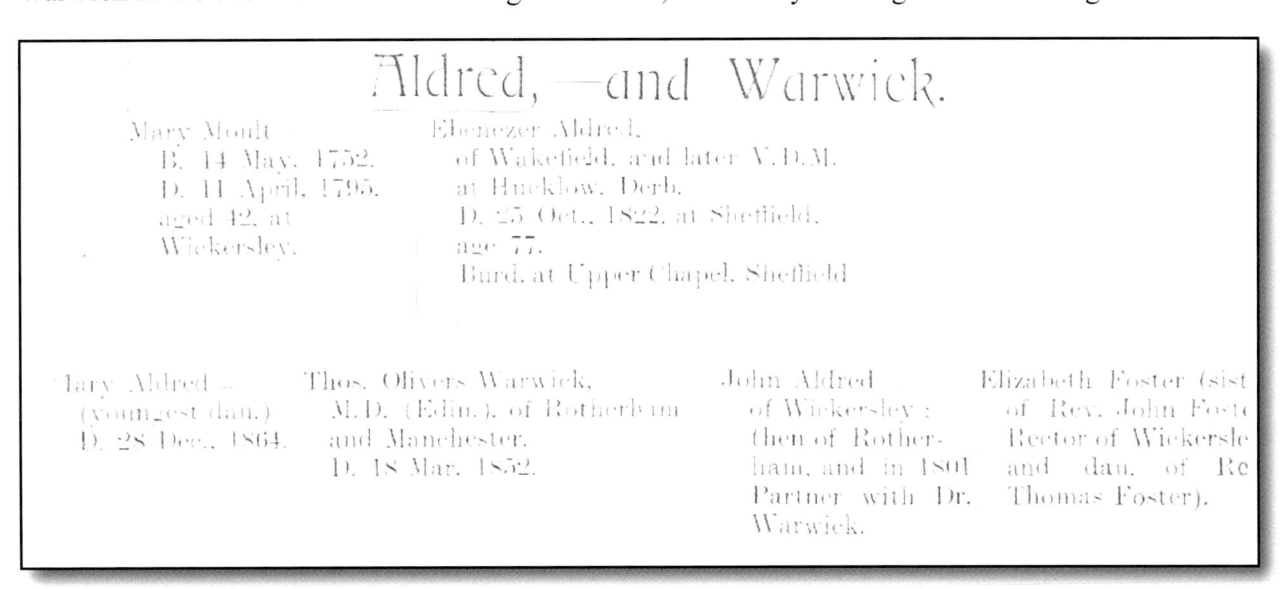

Aldred, —and Warwick.

Mary Moult
B. 14 May. 1752.
D. 11 April, 1795.
aged 42, at
Wickersley.

Ebenezer Aldred,
of Wakefield, and later V.D.M.
at Hucklow, Derb.
D. 25 Oct., 1822, at Sheffield,
age 77.
Burd. at Upper Chapel, Sheffield

Mary Aldred =
(youngest dau.)
D. 28 Dec., 1864.

Thos. Olivers Warwick,
M.D. (Edin.), of Rotherham
and Manchester.
D. 18 Mar. 1852.

John Aldred
of Wickersley;
then of Rotherham, and in 1801
Partner with Dr.
Warwick.

Elizabeth Foster (sist
of Rev. John Fost
Rector of Wickersle
and dau. of Re
Thomas Foster).

The above shows the family connection between John Aldred and Dr Warwick

John Aldred is buried in St Albans Churchyard, Wickersley where his epitaph reads he 'died in the faith of Christ and in charity with all men'.

[additional information about John Aldred can be found in Chapter 3 Wellgate House]

Tooker Road Samuel Tooker 1736-1806.

Samuel Tooker lived at Moorgate Hall which was purchased by his ancestor Charles Tooker in 1627. He was a Barrister and Recorder of Doncaster for thirty-one years and one of the foremost advocates in Yorkshire. Samuel played an active role as a magistrate and was as distinguished 'in law and estate management as he was in goodness and benevolence'.

In 1780 Samuel was listed as a Feoffee of the Common Lands of Rotherham. John Guest records that 'Mr Tookers name became so distinguished that Moorgate-road was called 'Tuckers Lane'.

From 1617-1788 the Feoffees on behalf of the people of Rotherham paid the Duke of Norfolk, as Lord of the Manor of Whiston the sum of four gold nobles [£1.6.8d] each year for 'chiminge' money or liberty of passage from the Mile Oaks to the top of Rotherham Moor. This was a more direct route instead of turning downhill at the Mile Oaks towards Wellgate in 'zig zag fashion' where the pack-horse road crossed fields at an angle into Wellgate.

The 'chymyage' money was a source of dispute with the Duke and in 1788 Samuel Tooker on behalf of the Feoffees had the yearly payment rescinded for the sum of £25.

Samuel was also well known for growing cabbages. Arthur Young, on a six month tour studying the agriculture of the north of England in the 1760's visited Samuel Tooker, and wrote in his book of his large crop of cabbages weighing 10lb-30lb each. Samuel had three acres of land and Young estimated that one acre would hold five thousand cabbages.

Richard Holden a distinguished solicitor and Jane Woodcock the niece of bachelor Samuel Tooker were married in 1792 and lived at Moorgate Hall with him. Richard was an accomplished artist and filled Moorgate Hall with his paintings.

Gerard Road Henry Gerard Hoare 1828-1896

Rev Charles James Hoare born 1781 in London married Jane Isabella Holden, daughter of Richard Holden of Moorgate, Rotherham in 1811. They had seven children, one of whom was Henry Gerard Hoare.

His father Rev C J Hoare was an evangelical Church of England clergyman who eventually became vicar of Blandford Forum, Dorsetshire. In 1821 he moved to the family living of Godstone near Reigate, Surrey and in 1829 became Archdeacon of Winchester. By 1930 there had been a Hoare as Rector of Godstone for 109 years.

Henry Gerard Hoare was related to Samuel Tooker through his mother's family.His ancestor Sir Richard Hoare founded a banking business dating back to Charles11.

In the 1920's twenty five new churches were wanted within the Diocese of Southwark. Uvedale and Cecily Lambert [nee Hoare] owned a 17th century barn in Oxted, Surrey, they no longer used and offered it as one of these churches. The barn was dismantled, each plank numbered, moved and re built at a cost of £5000, becoming Kew, St Philip & All Saints [The Barn Church].

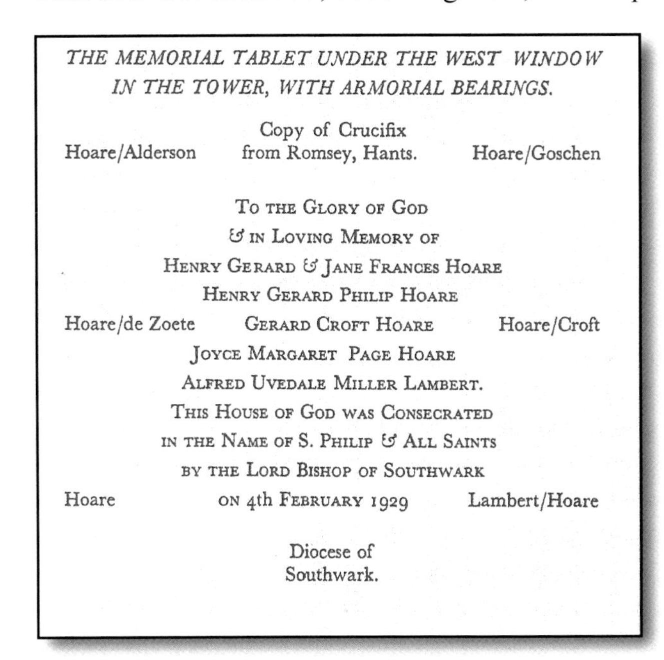
THE MEMORIAL TABLET UNDER THE WEST WINDOW IN THE TOWER, WITH ARMORIAL BEARINGS.

Hoare/Alderson — Copy of Crucifix from Romsey, Hants. — Hoare/Goschen

TO THE GLORY OF GOD
& IN LOVING MEMORY OF
HENRY GERARD & JANE FRANCES HOARE
HENRY GERARD PHILIP HOARE
Hoare/de Zoete — GERARD CROFT HOARE — Hoare/Croft
JOYCE MARGARET PAGE HOARE
ALFRED UVEDALE MILLER LAMBERT.
THIS HOUSE OF GOD WAS CONSECRATED
IN THE NAME OF S. PHILIP & ALL SAINTS
BY THE LORD BISHOP OF SOUTHWARK
Hoare — ON 4th FEBRUARY 1929 — Lambert/Hoare

Diocese of Southwark.

The Hoare family donated several interior furnishings and the Church was dedicated to the memory of Henry Gerard Hoare and other members of his family.

On 31st December 1870 a conveyance was made between Henry Gerard Hoare and Eliza Shore widow of Offley Shore [a close relative of Florence Nightingales father Mr William Shore Nightingale] regarding land in Moorgate. In a further conveyance to the Trustees of the Rotherham Charity, [Hollis Trust] two pieces of land in Godstone Road on 31st July 1894.

Godstone Road would also seem to have acquired its name from the Hoare family.

Mrs Hoare of Godstone Rectory presented a painting of a group of Cavalry and Infantry volunteers on Brinsworth Common dated 1804, to the Mechanics Institute. The painting shows a review of troops by Earl Fitzwilliam and Colonel Althorpe, also pictured are Joshua and Thomas Walker. This was painted by her father, Richard Holden, a lawyer, judge and artist who resided with his uncle, Samuel Tooker at Moorgate Hall. Holden was Captain of the Rotherham Troop of West Yeomanry Cavalry under the command of Colonel FF Foljambe.

[The painting can be viewed in Clifton Park Museum.]

Living at 'Netherleigh' **Gerard Road, James Totty** was one of the best known Architects and Surveyors in Rotherham. He was born 8th August 1869 and educated at the Borough Collegiate School. James was articled to Edwin Isle-Hubbard who founded the practice in 1859 and remained a pupil and assistant 1889-1904. From early work mainly for ecclesiastical and domestic clients he developed a more commercial client base, local to the Rotherham area.

In May 1904 James commenced his own business in Moorgate Street and built up a very successful practice. He had a wide reputation outside Rotherham and was responsible for many architectural schemes.

Following a fire on 25th February 1921, The Whitehall Cinema in High Street was rebuilt to a design by James Totty and re opened 7th January 1924. He was also responsible for designing a stone based memorial with two bronze plaques by the Lychgate at Whiston Parish Church.

The business increased and developed from its original Rotherham base and transferred to Sheffield becoming known as 'James Totty Partnership'.

Records for the County Borough of Rotherham 1897-1948 lists 246 architectural plans for James Totty.

Broom Valley

Plans were drawn up in 1938 for the new Broom Valley Estate showing the layout of the roads and houses to be built off Wellgate.

Rotherham Corporation applied for a compulsory purchase order of land at Broom Valley to provide much needed housing. At an Inquiry held in August 1948 objections were received from owners and occupiers of the land, but having dismissed an alternative site at Kimberworth Park, Broom Valley was deemed the best option.

At the entrance to Broom Valley the 'fish pond' was still showing on the 1938 housing plans [see chapter 3 Memories of an Earlier Time] In 1949 there were plans for a sub station at this site and by 1953-1954 the adjacent land was occupied by Bywater Funeral Directors.

In 1981 **Bartholomew & Sons Funeral Directors** took over the company and premises of Bywater and enlarged it by adding a chapel and office accommodation in 1991.

The business was established in 1891 by Alfred Bartholomew in Whiston. Prior to this from 1874 -1881 he was apprenticed to Benjamin Shepherd.

INDENTURE 23RD March 1874

Between **Alfred Bartholomew** of Whiston and **Benjamin Shepherd** of Guilthwaite, in the parish of Whiston in the said County, Wheelwright and Joiner.

Alfred Bartholomew with the consent of his father William Bartholomew bound himself Apprentice to Benjamin Shepherd for a term of seven years. He agreed to serve his master faithfully, keep his secrets, observe his lawful commands, forbear to do him harm, hurt or injury either to his person or property and to attend regularly and diligently to his affairs and interests. He would in every respect conduct himself as an industrious and trustworthy apprentice.

Benjamin Shepherd for his part agreed to teach and instruct Alfred in the trade or business of Wheelwright and Joiner. He would provide 'good and sufficient meat', drink and lodgings suitable for an apprentice and agreed to bear the expense of medicines and medical attendance in case of sickness or lameness.

Benjamin Shepherd would also provide 'good and proper clothes and wearing apparel, washing and mending of clothes. Alfred Bartholomew for his part would conduct himself as an honest and industrious apprentice during the said term.

Signed William Bartholomew
Alfred Bartholomew
Benjamin Shepherd

In 1891 **Alfred Bartholomew** became Wheelwright, Joiner and Undertaker in Whiston and was followed by his son **William James** in the family business. His sons **Dennis Gordon** and **William Philip** became the third generation of Funeral Directors in 1946.

Dennis was also very involved in the life of Whiston being a parish councillor for 40 years until 1995. He led the fight to protect the green belt in and around Whiston and involved himself in all aspects of village life. He will perhaps be best remembered for helping to save the Manorial Barn and was awarded the MBE for services to Whiston.

Tony Bartholomew continued the family tradition taking over Bywater Funeral Directors in Broom Valley in 1981 and was there until his retirement in 2008. His son **James** took over the running of the business and became the fifth generation of Bartholomew and Sons.

Adjacent is **Clarkson Monumental Mason**. The original company dates back to 1867 and their premises were in Effingham Street. The 1901 Rotherham Annual shows Clarkson & Co [Late I Hanby] Monumental Masons & Co

Isaac Hanby presented this font to Church of Our Father, Moorgate upon the opening of the church in 1880.

Clarkson's applied for planning permission in September 1965 for use of garages as Monumental Masons, showroom, office and workshop and moved to Broom Valley. Bartholomew & Sons amalgamated with Clarkson Monumental Mason and moved to new premises in Moorgate 2018.

William Easton 1829-1889

William Easton was a well-known and highly regarded person in Rotherham. He managed the Chemical Works in Wellgate after the death of John Aldred, subsequently purchased the business and moved to live in the adjacent Wellgate House. He owned land in Wellgate as shown in the 1886 indenture of Rotherham Evangelical church.

He was a member of St Stephens Church, Eastwood and played a prominent role in public affairs. Easton was a member of the Board of Guardians and served on the Rotherham Burial Board for a number of years. He concerned himself with the work of the Rotherham Hospital and Dispensary and for two or three years held the position of Overseer to the Poor for Rotherham. In addition to these duties William Easton was also a director of the Equitable Investment and Loan Society and a Governor with the Rotherham Savings Bank. In private life he was always willing to give a helping hand.

Gummer gives an interesting insight into the area around and beyond Wellgate House in 1889. 'Gerard Road was not opened out, nor any street adjoining it. This part of Wellgate was said to be in the country. There were no houses after the Chemical Works except the Toll House until you came to Leedhams Farm'.

He also refers to William Easton as 'the old gentleman's impressive demeanour' He died aged 59 years!

Thomas Allport 1804-1879

Thomas Allport was born in Staffordshire and came to Rotherham in the 1830's. He married Sarah Thickett in 1849 at the Parish Church in Rotherham and they had three children. He was a Botanical and Landscape artist and exhibited five botanical drawings at the Liverpool Academy. He did some work as a lithographer and examples of this work are the two pictures of the Old Chapel Downs Row.

View of Rotherham from Bromley Sands 1850

1704-1841

1841-current

Whites Directory 1845 show him as a miniature painter and drawing master at Clifton Terrace and he is listed in the 1851 census as living in Wellgate with his family His son James inherited his artistic ability and was employed at Yates & Haywood as a designer.

Refs
Wellgate
Rotherham Archives & Local Studies Service
Kellys Directories 1901-1961
Guest John Historic Notices of Rotherham 1879
Rotherham Advertiser 25/2/2000

Photograph
Rotherham Family History Society George Bentley Collection
Cox's Buildings

Churchwardens plaque 1848
Information
Crowder Freda & Greene Dorothy Rotherham Its History, Church & Chapel on the Bridge 1971

Photograph
Ralph Jackson

Doncaster Gate
Rotherham Archives & Local Studies Service
Archive Catalogue 1-T to 44 RD 14/H
Various pamphlets Rotherham Hospital ref 942-741/362-1
Rotherham Its History & Its Work reprinted from Rotherham Advertiser 21/11/1903
Rotherham Advertiser 22/1/1870, 15/3/1924, 3/7/1948
Rotherham Annual 1913
Guest John Historic Notices of Rotherham 1879
Rotherham Hospital Annual Report 1935

Photographs
Rotherham Archives & Local Studies Service
Doncaster Gate 1903-1906 ref 6294 photographer unknown
Doncaster Gate Hospital - Philip H J Smedley
Rotherham Dispensary bottle - M A Croft
Hospital Ward Dr GB Peckitt, Nurse Jane Peckitt [nee Gillan] – Dr GB Peckitt
4 x 1st World War 1916/1917 Joan & Philip Graham
Life Governor Receipt W Mapplebeck
Cartoon Dr G B Peckitt

High Street - The Royal Bank of Scotland
Rotherham Archives & Local Studies Service
Whites Sheffield & District Directory 1884 Ref 942/74 SHE-ST
Rotherham Advertiser17/5/1890, 9/1/1892, 15/12/1906, 25/9/1970, 30/1/1954, 2/5/1964, 26/3/1966, 25/9/1970, 4/10/1985, 10/8/1990.
Who's Who File
Banking in Yorkshire by WCE Hartley ref 942.74/332-1
Photograph
R Jackson

Quarry Hill
Rotherham Archives & Local Studies Service
Rotherham Advertiser 28/9/1867, 2/10/1937, 17/1/1975, 11/8/2000

Photograph
Rotherham Archives & Local Studies Service
Vere Baker's Quarry Hill 1937 ref 05611 photographer Sheffield Telegraph LMA
Advertisement - Rotherham Advertiser 2/10/1937

Mansfield Road
Information
P H J Smedley,
John Hargreaves
Kellys 1881 Directory, Rotherham Annual 1911 – John Hargreaves
Rotherham Archives & Local Studies Service
Rotherham Advertiser 2/4/1904, 7/10/1912
Bockley Agnes, Callear Veronica Wellgate Old Hall
Kellys Directories

Photographs
Looking down Mansfield Road RFHS Colin Leonard Collection 1964
Petrol Pump M Jackson. Courtesy South Yorkshire Transport Museum
Barn, Kimbers, Hargreaves, P H J Smedley
Barn & Demolition x5 P H J Smedley
Barn demolition John Hargreaves
Looking up Mansfield Road P H J Smedley
Kimbers Advertisement & Soft Drinks labels John Hargreaves

Hargreaves Plumbers
Information
John Hargreaves

Photograph
M Jackson

Albion Road [William Street]
Rotherham Archives & Local Studies Service
J S Crowther Press Cuttings 1958-1980, 1981-1992, 942-741/920 CRO
Rotherham Advertiser 26/5/1995
Crowther Stan Autobiography 'One Thing After Another' 2005

Photograph
Pauline & Michael Bentley Collection
Albion Road 1912

Hollowgate
Information
Rotherham Archives & Local Studies Service
Whittington & Whittington Blacksmith 1859 ref 63-B/5/A/23

Photograph
Rotherham Archives & Local Studies Service
Hollowgate 1937 ref 08667 photographer unknown

Vicarage Lane
Rotherham Archives & Local Studies Service
Information ref 790 - F, F/2, F/3, F/4, F/5.
Rotherham Advertiser 21/3/1931, 28/3/1931, 3/5/1958, 10/1/1975, 31/1/1975

Photographs
Rotherham Archives & Local Studies Service
Adams Brothers 1931 ref 10297 photographer unknown LMA
Demolition of Henry Adams house x 2 P H J Smedley

Sherwood Crescent
Information
Rotherham Archives & Local Studies Service
Rotherham Advertiser 1/12/1883

Photographs
R Jackson

Narrow Twitchell
Photographs
RFHS Colin Leonard Collection 1964
The original Signage John Hargreaves - Photograph M Jackson

Spinners Walk
Information
Rotherham Past & Present Munford AP 2001
Photograph
Rotherham Family History Society
Colin Leonard Collection 1965

Pinfold Lane
Rotherham Archives & Local Studies Service
Guest John Historic Notices of Rotherham 1879
Munford A P History of Rotherham 2000
Rotherham Advertiser 18/2/2000

Albany Street
Rotherham Archives & Local Studies Service
Who's Who File
Photographs
Bailey Bridge M Jackson
1920's Anonymous contribution - with thanks from the author

Warwick Street

Blazeby W Rev	Rotherham Old Meeting House & Its Ministers 1906

Aldred Street

Blazeby W Rev	Rotherham Old Meeting House & Its Ministers 1906
Crowder F, Greene D	Rotherham Its History Church & Chapel 1971

Tooker Road
Rotherham Archives & Local Studies Service
Cockburn JH Rotherham Lawyers during 350 years 1932 ref 942-741/340
Young Arthur Six Month Tour Vol 1 Letter 3 1769
Guest John Historic Notices of Rotherham 1879
Munford AP A History of Rotherham 2000
Crowder F, Greene D Rotherham 1971
Munford AP Victorian Rotherham 1989
Picture from A sketch of Mr Alderman John Guest by T Biggs 1881

Gerard Road /Godstone Road
Rotherham Archives & Local Studies Service
Rotherham Advertiser 19/5/2000
Guest John Historic Notices of Rotherham 1879 page 528
Cockburn J H Rotherham Lawyers during 350 year 1932 ref 942-741/340
Wikepedia Rev Charles James Hoare
Kew St Philips & All Saints [The Barn Church] Kew Surrey
Blomfield David Extract of Kew Past 1994
Lambert Uvedale Appendix The Barn Church of Saint Philip the Apostle & All Saints 1936
Picture of Tablet taken from the above

James Totty
Rotherham Archives & Local Studies Service
Information Rotherham Annual 1920-1945
Sally Shepard-Archivist
Internet information-James Totty Partnership

Broom Valley
Rotherham Archives & Local Studies Service
1938 Broom Valley Plans
Rotherham Advertiser 21/8/1948
Planning fiche for Wellgate
Rotherham Annual 1901
Kellys Directories
Information
Bartholomew & Sons - Tony Bartholomew
Isaac Hanby – Margaret Jackson

Photographs
R & M Jackson

William Easton
Rotherham Archives & Local Studies Service
Rotherham Advertiser 30/3/1889 page 3
Gummers Reminiscences of Rotherham 1927
Indenture 1886 Rotherham Evangelical Church

Thomas Allport
1851 census
Internet Information
Pictures Old Chapel Downs Row-Rotherham Old Meeting House Blazeby W 1906
Bromley Sands Postcard loaned by D & J Clennell

Advertisement
Crowthers Stores Rotherham Advertiser 15/12/1906.

CROWTHER'S STORES,
Wiltshire House, 86, Wellgate,
CORNER OF MANSFIELD ROAD.
FAMILY ORDERS A SPECIALITY.
We are now offering, for which we have been many years noted, our
CHRISTMAS STILTONS.
RICH and CREAMY or RIPE BLUE.
FINEST CHEESE DIRECT FROM CHESHIRE.
CROWTHER'S FINEST AMERICAN (Rich Toasters).
CROWTHER'S NOTED GORGONZOLAS.
CROWTHER'S HOME FED HAMS and BACON.
CROWTHER'S SMOKED HAMS and BACON.
CROWTHER'S DANISH BUTTER is Perfection.
CROWTHER'S are noted for Best COOKING EGGS and FRESH EGGS for Boiling.
All Orders by Post will receive Prompt Attention.
WILTSHIRE HOUSE, ROTHERHAM.
Stiltons, Home-fed Hams, Smoked Hams for Christmas Presents, packed in small hampers and sent to any address required.

Chapter 6
Shops and Businesses

Wellgate was a busy thoroughfare with a mix of individual shops providing much of what the customer required. Many traders had served the public for several years and were household names.

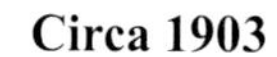

Circa 1903

Joseph Crowther

Joseph Crowther was born in 1851. He appears in the 1901 Kellys Directory as a Provisions Merchant and India Tea Blender & boot dealer at 12-14 Church Street. By 1903 he is also listed at 86 Wellgate as a Grocer.

From 1905 the business continued in Wellgate and in 1908 is listed as Joseph Crowther & Son, Grocers.

The Crowther family were astute business people and had the above picture reproduced onto postcards. Their customers wrote orders on the reverse side thus advertising the shop.

Joseph Crowther died in 1916 and the business continued with his elder son George W Crowther who died in 1948. Crowther's Stores ceased trading in 1961.

The top picture shows George Crowther in the doorway with his father Joseph in the background. The little boy by the horse and cart is Cyril Joseph Crowther who would become the father of Joseph Stanley Crowther, Member of Parliament for Rotherham 1976-1992.

A new building, built on the site of the Pack Horse Inn at the corner of Wellgate and Doncaster Gate.

In the late 1950's it was known as Van Allan Ltd, Ladies Outfitters. A fashion shop but also remembered by people of a 'certain age' as 'Van Allan's Corner', a meeting place.

Ref 11024 Circa 1907

This picture shows Van Allan fashion shop, J R Lloyd Opticians, D & J S Wilson, China and Glassware shop, Appleby & Miles, Drapers.

D & J S Wilson re located to Wellgate from Church Street when the site was demolished to give a better view of The Parish Church.

After the Second World War customers were able to join a savings club in Appleby & Miles to buy nylon stockings. Next door a passage led behind the shops to a small courtyard with cottages.

ALLIED FACILITIES

For THEATRE TICKETS (Sheffield and Leeds), BUTLIN'S HOLIDAY CAMPS, COACH BOOKINGS, TAXI HIRE, CHROMIUM PLATING, LIGHTER PARTS, Etc., Etc.

23 WELLGATE **ROTHERHAM**

At Allied Facilities you could book seats for the Sheffield Empire Shows.
Stalls 3/6d per seat plus 3d Booking Fee.

RFHS Colin Leonard Collection **1961**

The changing face of Wellgate

RFHS Colin Leonard Collection **1969**

Miss Pearson, a high-class establishment with assistants eager to please prospective buyers. Above the frontage of the building are lovely decorations in stonework and a plaque stating 1904. The shop is now occupied by Terry English, Optician.

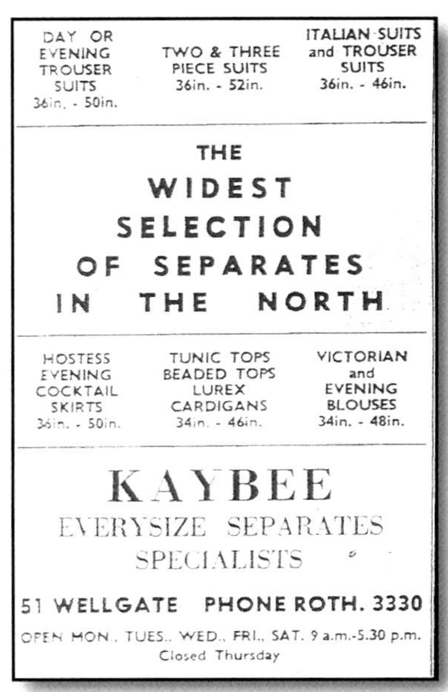

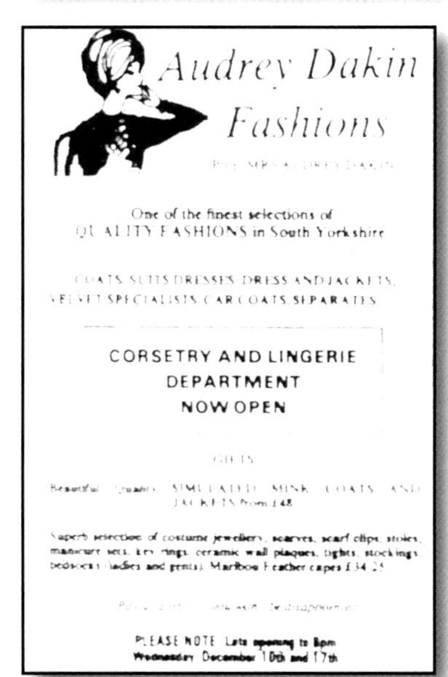

Gentlemen were also catered for in Wellgate with David Price, O & J Waters, J W Sellars and Wilfred Hill

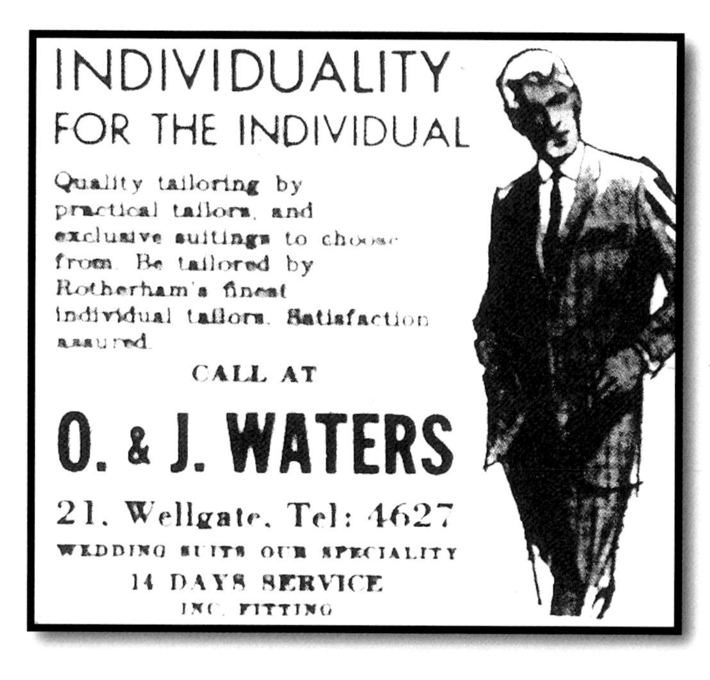

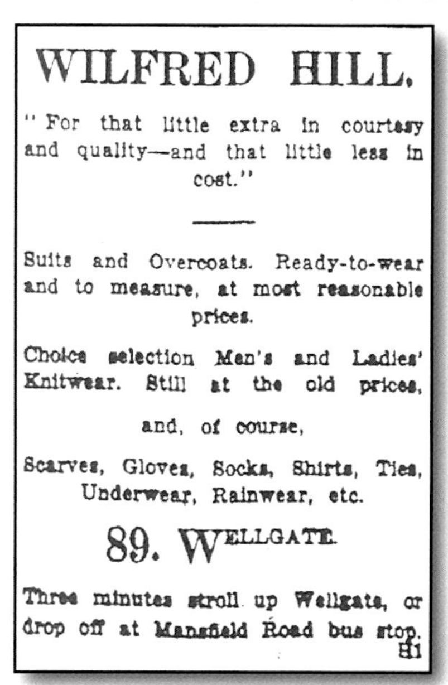

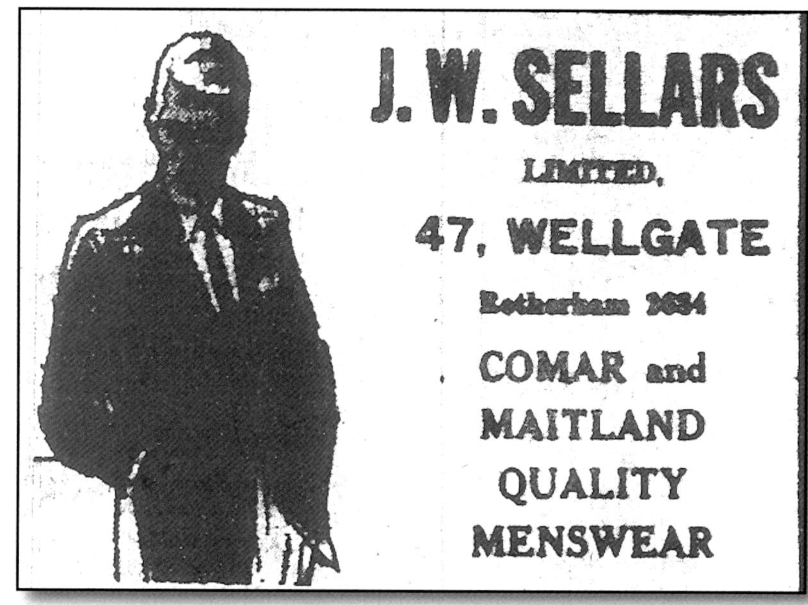

Wilfred Hill began his career with the Bradford Shipping Trade working wholesale dealing with different types of fabric. Moving to a Leeds company he became a buyer of furs and children's clothes. Following this he worked for a Leicester firm starting a children's clothing department and then became assistant buyer for a mail order company in Manchester.

Wilfred Hill and his family moved to Rotherham in 1945/6 and lived in Ramsden Road. He came as a store manager for Gillings followed by working from home selling farming clothes [ie plus fours], mail order. He moved into made to measure and bespoke tailoring using the front room of his house as a showroom.

In 1949 Wilfred Hill opened a men's outfitting shop in Wellgate and the family moved to live on the premises. He expanded the business across the road to 78/80 Wellgate as a Tailoring shop whilst outfitting remained at 89 Wellgate. By 1959 the business transferred to Frederick Street taking over G P Merifield & Son, Tailors. In 1961 he opened another shop at 23 Corporation Street.

The business continued at both premises until 1970 when the Frederick Street branch was demolished for the new bus station. Wilfred Hill, Outfitters continued in Corporation Street until the demolition of All Saints Buildings.

Mr Charles Denham Snr moved to the Wellgate premises in 1948/9. After leaving school at 14 years old he initially worked in a Pawn Shop in Broad Street, Parkgate and then at Gummers Brass Founders. He moved to Parkgate Iron & Steel at the age of 17 and progressed through the company eventually becoming Traffic Manager.

In 1946 he resigned his job to devote time to the family business in Parkgate selling household goods and kitchenware.

By 1949 he moved to the Wellgate shop and began to specialise in China and Glass, later selling lighting and lampshades. His daughter Mrs Doreen Nicholls managed the shop until its closure. Her artistic flair drew customers to view the shop windows especially at Christmastime.

In 1996 the shop changed hands and in 2002 a new tearoom opened above the shop. The business closed in 2003.

RFHS Colin Leonard Collection 1964

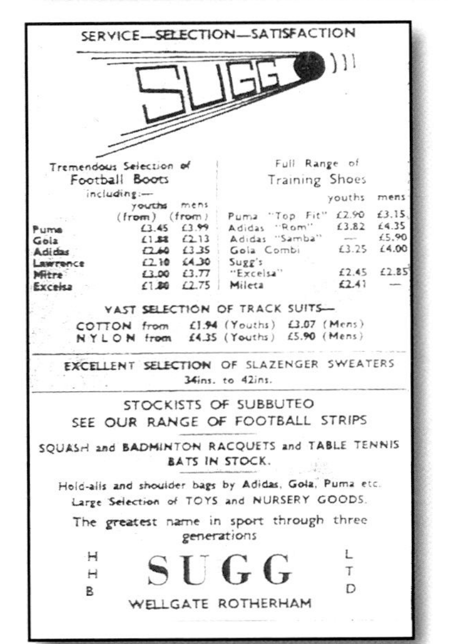

H.H.B Sugg Ltd opened a branch in Wellgate in the mid 1950's. The original premises were quite cramped but they acquired an adjoining shop which enabled them to separate their goods into two departments. One sold radios, television and household electrical appliances and the other department dealt with sports accessories. The shop eventually concentrated on sports related goods until closure in 2001.

Edwin Clover – High Class Fish Purveyor

E & A Clover winning 1st prize in the Rotherham Shopping Week Competition 1926

Pictured Edwin Clover Albert Clover
Son Edwin Clover Asst Henry Jarvis

Edwin Clover & Sons

HIGH-CLASS FISH PURVEYOR

AGENT FOR PALETHORPES SAUSAGES
LICENSED GAME DEALER

19 Wellgate Rotherham

Telephone 5364 and 5365

After the 1st World War the Clover family moved to Rotherham from Sheffield and lived on Clifton Bank, off Wellgate.

Edwin Clover purchased a business from Mr C Woodcock, Fishmonger, situated in High Street [next to the Maypole].

Subsequently Muntus bought the property for expansion of their store and Clovers relocated to Wellgate in 1923.

Sons Edwin and Arthur joined the family business in Wellgate after leaving school and younger brother Douglas followed some years later when he left school.

In 1930 Clovers opened another shop at 245 Doncaster Road, East Dene run by Edwin until the Second World War intervened. Douglas and his brother Arthur were called up for National service, Douglas into the Army, serving in the Middle East and Arthur into the RAF.

Because of shortage of supplies of fish due to the sea warfare and lack of available staff, the East Dene shop was sold in 1942 and the business continued in Wellgate.

Arthur was killed during the war but Douglas returned and went back into the business in 1946. Father Edwin, born 1888 retired from the shop in 1948 and sons Douglas and Edwin carried on the business until 1977 when the shop closed.

After retiring Douglas went to work at the head office of the Trustee Savings Bank in Sheffield 1977-1984 and 'enjoyed every minute of it'.

Orly Travel

In 1963 **Kenneth Harder DFC** moved from London to Rotherham to set up the business of Orly Travel Ltd at 33 Wellgate. His family followed in January 1964.

Mr Harder held executive positions in the travel trade since 1947 and was a member of the Institute of Travel Tourism. In 1965 he was invited to become Managing Director of the Company.

The business transferred to 37 Wellgate in 1971.

Mr Harder visited China in December 1980 as part of the European Travel Trade Mission to China.

During World War Two he served with the RAF gaining the Distinguished Flying Cross.

Mr Harder retired in 1984 and subsequently published a book entitled

'The Key to Survival'
Bomber Command in World War Two.

Harrison Proctor Studios were situated in the Cleaver Buildings and specialised in wedding and portrait photography. They had a picture framing business and sold paintings, greeting cards and old sepia photographs. In 1984 they moved to 81 Wellgate until closure in 2001/2002.

RFHS Colin Leonard Collection **1962**

On the right is **Wellgate Post Office**. Above, the bay windows can still be seen but the adjacent houses have disappeared. Next to the Post Office was Holgans Shoe shop.

In 1866 a 'Town Auxiliary Letter Carrier' served an eight mile radius six days per week including Wellgate and departed Rotherham Head Office 7am.

1964

A wall letter box opened in Wellgate in 1872 with 296 letters posted during the first three weeks of use.

In April 1882 the forerunner of Wellgate Post Office known as Broom Road 'Town Receiving Office' opened near Sherwood Crescent with Morris Brettell as Receiver.

The office opened daily except Sunday 7am-9pm. Letters were dispatched to Head Office 10.40am, 4.50pm and 8.20pm. A Receiving Office accepted letters but did not deliver.

The Post Office renamed Wellgate Town Sub Office moved to its present position in Wellgate and opened 1st November 1952.

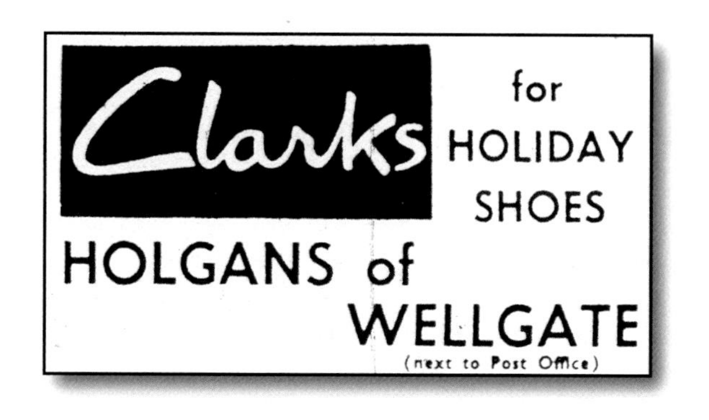

The corner of Sherwood Crescent

For many years from the beginning of the twentieth century 121 Wellgate on the corner of Sherwood Crescent has been used as a Drapery shop.

Maurice Creswick, Draper, is listed there from 1901-1912. From 1916-1927 **Francis Dunford, Draper** was there and the sign above the shop can still be seen. In addition to Drapery the shop was also used as a Post Office in the mid twentieth century.

It continued as a Drapery shop in the late 1960's with Amy McCartin at 119 Wellgate.

Dunford Wellgate Hosiery Drapery Stores

MARY REANEY
LADIES FASHIONS

For Cocktail and Formal Wear, Stylish Blouses Day Dresses, Suits for all occasions including the latest styles in Velour
Personal Attention

1980

In the 1970's and early 1980's Mary Reaney was listed as Draper at 119 & 121 Wellgate.

RFHS[PT] Colin Leonard Collection 1964
Entrance to Fred Elliott Ltd House Furnishers

Fred Elliott began his furniture business in 1931 with a shop at the top of Bridgegate, in the White Hart Buildings, selling new furniture.

In 1932 he opened a second hand warehouse in the Cleaver Yard, Wellgate. The business expanded and another shop opened in 1938 at 23 Wellgate selling a large selection of three piece suites in Dermide and Leather cloth from £8.12.6d. Bedroom suites in oak or walnut cost £8.17.6d and Dining tables cost from £1.19.6d.

The Elliott family consisted of eleven children and most of them were employed in the business. Fred junior [known as Jack] worked in Wellgate until the Second World War intervened. He was called up for national service in July 1940, followed by his younger brothers.

After the war they returned to the business with Ronald Elliott working in Wellgate. By 1954 another shop opened at 10 -14 Bridgegate. This shop was taken over by Jas Woodhouse & Sons in 1961 and Elliotts transferred their two Bridgegate businesses to the Tivoli. The Cleaver Yard business continued until the 1970's.

Fred Elliott 1940

Fred Elliott was one of the first people in Rotherham to own a Rolls Royce.
The vehicle is pictured in Ramsden Road.
Circa 1945.

Bygone Hairdressers

RFHS Colin Leonard Collection 1961

The shop of Les Blaireaux hairdresser is just visible to the right of this picture at 26 Wellgate from 1961-1968 and was located at 24 & 29 Wellgate in 1974. 'Lucille' was at 29 Wellgate 1957-1971.

RFHS Colin Leonard 1964 [pt]

Other hairdressers in Wellgate for a number of years were: **Ivy Payne 1938-1964**

Ivy Payne
Ladies' & Children's Hairdresser
12a WELLGATE. PHONE. 3461.
Wireless and Machineless Curly Perms our Speciality
Several other systems to choose from
EXPERT HAIR STYLIST

Sheila Pashley remembers a cut, shampoo and set costing eight shillings 'which was quite expensive at the time'. After the closure of 'Ivy Payne, Denham's expanded their shop taking over these premises.

Patricia Kellett
70 Wellgate
1959 –1963 moved to 61 Wellgate and was still there in 1974.

Patricia Kellett
Ladies' Hairdresser
of Distinction
70 Wellgate, Rotherham
Telephone 78073. Phone for Appointment

Modern day hairdressers included Peter Bird at 6B Wellgate from 1998 until 2012 when they transferred to Corporation Street.

178 Wellgate

Hardware shop - Proprietor Rose Ann Wright.

Greengrocers shop - Proprietors Charles Henry & Sally Wright C H Wright is listed from 1908-1951.

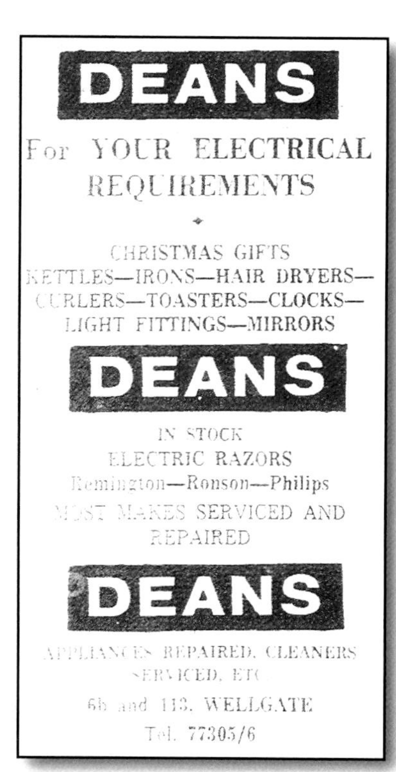

Deans Electrical 113 Wellgate

Deans Electrical Company was situated in Nottingham Street Circa 1919 and owned by Jack and Harry Dean. Roland Cutts eventually took over the business followed by Brian and Graham Cutts. Brian 'headed the company' from 1980.

The business transferred to Wellgate in 1963 and was opened by Alderman Duffield.

The premises consisted of a trade and retail outlet with offices on two floors. Behind the shop was a workshop. Deans had a reputation for the design and installation of electrical systems.

In 1993 Deans Electrical and Engineering and its subsidiary Electrical Testing Services was taken over by the Rex group of companies.

Mr **Robert Henry Thickett** was a Butcher, Farmer, Cattle Dealer and Dairyman. He farmed at Wickersley and Herringthorpe on land that is now known as Herringthorpe Playing Fields. By 1939 Kellys directory lists him as a farmer at Munsbro' Hall Farm, Greasbro.

In 1898 he is listed as a butcher at 12 The Shambles, living in Wickersley and in 1901 he had butchers shops at 179 Wellgate and 2 The Shambles. He was at 19 Doncaster Gate in 1908 and by 1916 was listed as a butcher and dairyman at 6 Wellgate. The business continued in Wellgate and was still there in 1974.

RFHS Colin Leonard Collection 1964

F L Smith Electrical Engineer appears in Kellys Directories 1936 at 119 Wellgate.

In 1948 he moved to 9a Wellgate and was there until 1961.

The heyday of his business was in the 1950's when television arrived and he either sold or rented them to customers.

In addition to 9A Wellgate the rear and upstairs of 22 Wellgate was used as an office and base for his contracting and repair business with family member Jack Pearson as office manager.

When the owner of 9A Wellgate leased the building to the Trustee Savings Bank F.L.Smith transferred temporarily behind 24 Wellgate in 1962 before moving into his new shop at 6B Wellgate Chambers in 1963 and is listed there until 1972.

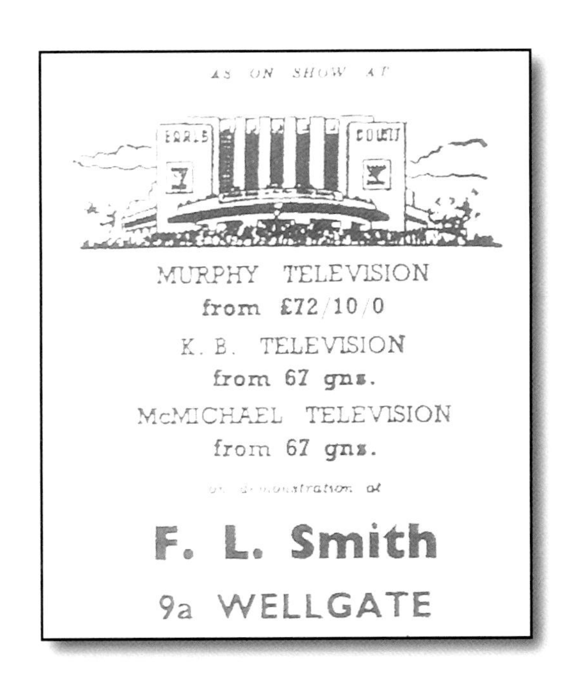

Hagues Newsagents

Ref 00185 **1939**

Just visible below the grocery van of H S Bristowe is the clock over the premises of **Bob Hague, Newsagent**. Born in 1908 he was in business as a Newsagent and Tobacconist at 216 Wellgate from 1933-1974 and at 212 Wellgate from 1935-1974 as a shopkeeper. He was also at 222 Wellgate listed as a Fancy Draper from1938 until the early 1950's.

Mr Hague was a member of the National Federation of Retail Newsagents and President of the local branch three times, President of the Rotherham Chamber of Trade and President and Treasurer of Rotherham Neptunas Swimming Club.

He served as Chairman of the Rotherham Independent and Progressive Party and although he unsuccessfully contested the Clifton Ward Municipal Elections in 1952 was elected as Independent Councillor for the South Ward in 1953, a position he held until 1974.

Another popular newsagent in Wellgate was **Richardson's**.

Cyril Richardson joined the family newsagents business started by his grandfather in Wellgate in 1867, at the age of 15. He worked there until the Second World War commenced and left to join the army. In 1945 he returned and took over the business and remained in Wellgate until his retirement in1980.

His sons continued the business in Wickersley and the Stag.

He was a supporter of Rotherham United Football Club and a member of the Fellowship of the Services Bailey Bridge 186 Mess.

Ye Old Gate Café 1948-1961 became Golden Swallow 1963-1970

Ye Old Gate Cafe
(Prop. R. P. FULLER)
PARTIES and WEDDINGS CATERED FOR
ESTIMATES FREE
36–38 WELLGATE ROTHERHAM
Phone: Rotherham 541511

1952

For Quality . . .
NUTS—DRIED FRUITS—HONEY—
CEREALS and all HEALTH FOOD and
HERBAL REQUIREMENTS
VISIT
THE Health Food Store
26, WELLGATE

1971

NORMAN SPEIGHT
WHOLESALE & RETAIL TRIPE PURVEYOR
20 WELLGATE
and 63 Frederick Street
ROTHERHAM

Speight's, Purveyors of Tripe started their business in 1884 and since then five generations of the family have been involved.

They had several shops including Wellgate and Parkgate and market stalls in Doncaster and Mexborough.

In 1980 planning permission was granted for a new factory to be built close to their Parkgate shop after a compulsory purchase order was served on the original premises. The tripe was prepared for sale in the factory and sold in their various shops. Memories of their Wellgate shop include tripe, chitterling, bag, udder and cow heels usually referred to as 'coweels'. In 1994 the family announced the closure of their business due to ill health.

"For a meal that satisfies even me I go to . . ."
RICKSHAW RESTAURANT
31, WELLGATE, ROTHERHAM
Telephone 77502
ENGLISH and CHINESE CUISINE
Businessman's 3-course lunch
Served Daily 3/6
FULLY LICENSED UNTIL 11.30 p.m.
WE SPECIALISE IN CATERING FOR PARTIES
AND IN SERVING FOOD TO YOUR HOME
THE BEST IN TOWN

1961-1963

The **Rickshaw Restaurant** and Espresso Coffee Bar 1961-1963 changed to the Willow Garden Restaurant and later became 'Hong Kong' followed by The Golden Goddess Restaurant.

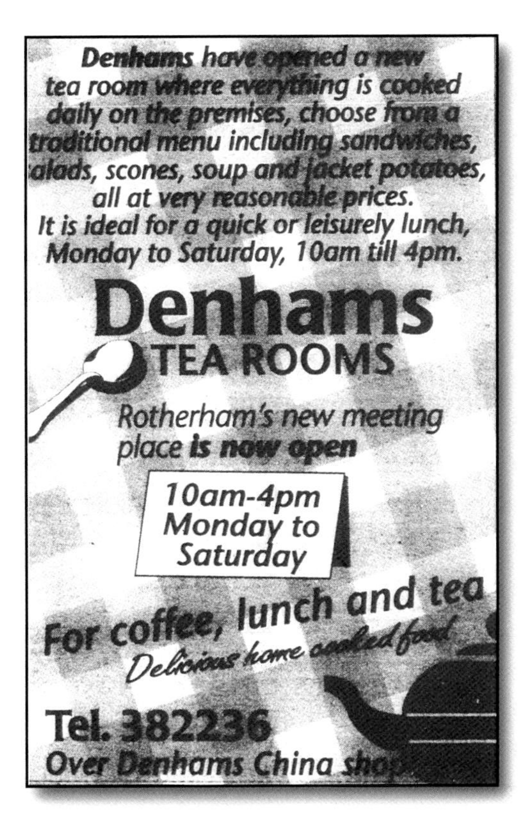

2002-2003

A Russell Esq Butchers 159A Wellgate

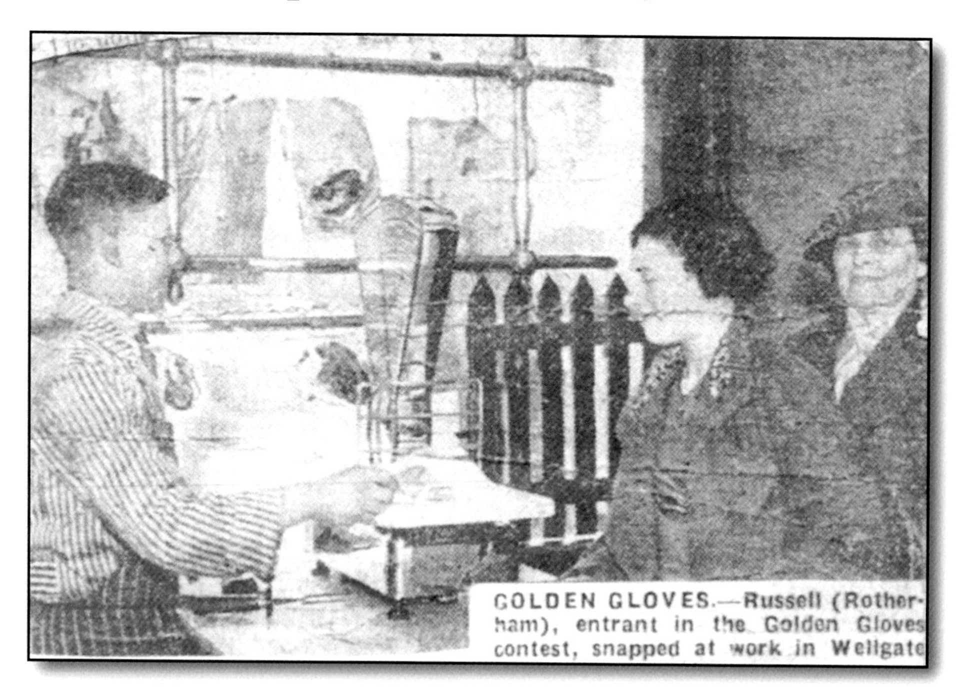
GOLDEN GLOVES.—Russell (Rotherham), entrant in the Golden Gloves contest, snapped at work in Wellgate

Alfred Russell, Master Butcher, was born in 1915. He started in the butchery trade after leaving school and is pictured here in his early twenty's serving customers in his shop in Wellgate.

Alfred and his family lived 'over the shop' rented from Bentleys Breweries.

His father Arthur Russell started a boys boxing club in Parkgate to 'encourage children off the streets'. His three sons, Alfred, Arthur and Raymond all became amateur boxing champions. Alfred won many championships including Amateur champion of North of England.

He represented Great Britain on 5th May 1936 in the Amateur Boxing Golden Gloves tournament against America at Wembley beating Joe Wall, from New York.

In June 1936 Alfred had the honour of being chosen to represent Great Britain at the 1936 Olympics in Berlin, Germany and received a letter of congratulations.

The X1 Olympiad was opened by Adolf Hitler 1st August 1936.

In 1938 Alfred was the ABA flyweight champion. The Second World War intervened and he was called up to serve in the Army.

The three Russell brothers Alfred, Arthur and Raymond were all butchers by trade but boxing was an important part of their leisure time.

Stockdales Fruiterers

Frank Stockdale, born in 1912 opened his first shop in 1935 in Wellgate. He continued the tradition started by his grandfather John Stockdale, born in 1846, and shown on the 1901 census as a Fruiterer.

Franks father Arthur was a Greengrocer who had six sons and a daughter. One of his sons Arthur was killed in the war and son John had a hawking round. The other brothers Sid, Jim, Frank and Albert all had businesses trading as the well known 'Stockdales Fruiterers' in the market, College Road, Kimberworth Park and Wellgate.

Daughter Margaret worked in the family business in town.

Frank lived with his family 'over the shop'. In 1940 he was called up for National Service in the Army. His wife Mary continued to run the shop in his absence until his return from the war.

In 1968 Frank opened a fruit shop in Broom Lane. After his death in 1970 the Wellgate shop was sold but Stockdales continued by opening a shop in Wickersley followed by a town centre shop in Effingham Street. After the Rotherham Advertiser site was demolished the shop relocated back to Wellgate and continued until the 1980's.

Frank Stockdale at the opening of his Wellgate shop in 1935

00184

These shops pre date the multi storey car park in Wellgate. The next shop to the Lyons Ice Cream advertisement is Ernest Giles, Opticians, who started their business here before moving lower down Wellgate.

1958

1925

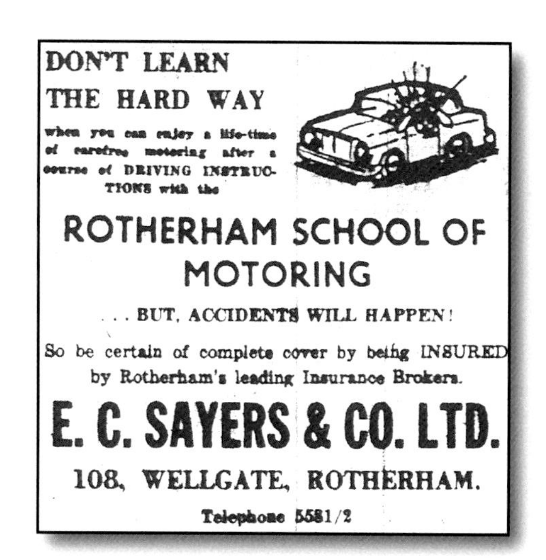

1965

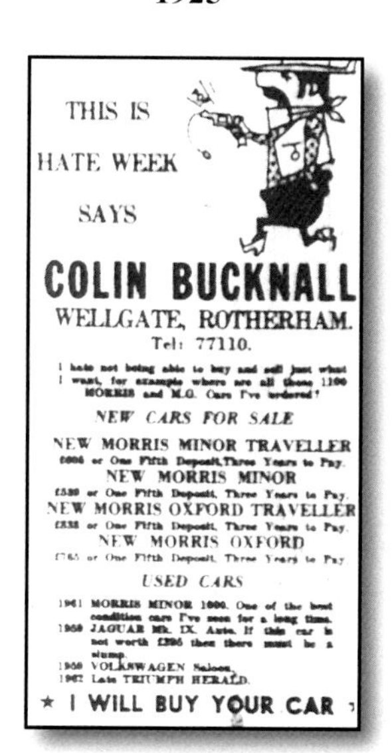

1964

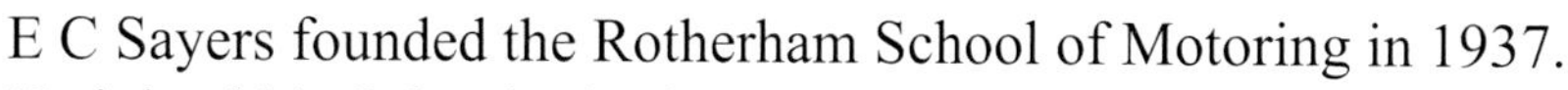

E C Sayers founded the Rotherham School of Motoring in 1937. He joined his father in the family business of E W Sayers & Sons, Insurance Agents [see photo chapter 7] in Wellgate in 1932 prior to starting his school of motoring five years later. He retired to Devon in 1968.

1952

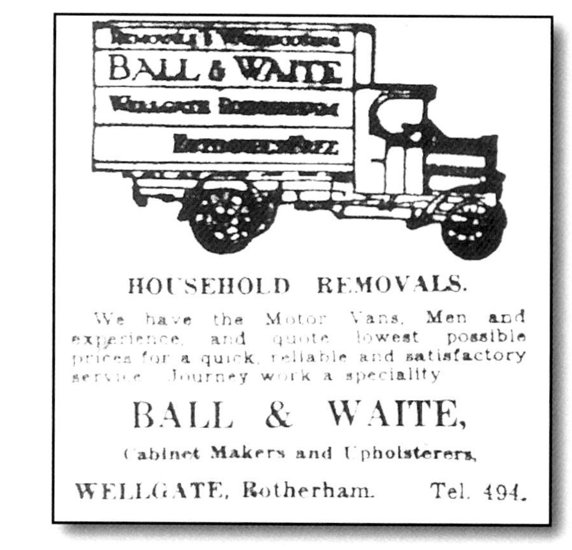

1935

REFS

Crowther's Stores
Information
Mr J S Crowther
Kellys Directories 1901, 1908, 1948, 1961.
Whites Directories 1903, 1905

Photographs
Mr J S Crowther
Crowthers Stores
Portrait of Joseph Crowther

Van Allan etc
Information
Van Allan, D & J S Wilson M Jackson
Appleby & Miles M Ramsden, Allied Facilities Ann Kirk

Photographs
Rotherham Archives & Local Studies Service
Site of the Pack Horse Inn Wellgate 1907 ref 11024
[Van Allan Ltd]
Rotherham Advertiser LMA

Photographs
Rotherham Family History Society
Changing Face of Wellgate[1]Colin Leonard Collection 1961
Changing Face of Wellgate [2] Colin Leonard Collection 1969

Wilfred Hill
Information
Mrs Christine Wilson
Rotherham Archives & Local Studies Service
Kellys Directories 1948, 1954, 1957, 1959, 1960, 1961.
Star 11/12/1963

Denham's
Information
Rotherham Archives & Local Studies Service
Rotherham Advertiser 8/6/1984, 24/2/1995, 25/1/2002,7/2/2003,
Mrs Doreen Nicholls
Mrs Kath Taylor

Photograph [pt]
Rotherham Family History Society
Denhams Colin Leonard Collection 1964

HHB Sugg Ltd
Rotherham Archives & Local Studies Service
Rotherham Advertiser 20/6/1959
Goad Maps 2000, 2001.

Edwin Clover
Information
Mr Douglas Clover
Rotherham Archives & Local Studies Service
Kellys Directories 1922, 1924, 1930, 1941, 1942.

Photograph
E & A Clover 1926
Mrs Pauline Thackray/ D Clover

Orly Travel
Information
Pippa Harder
Rotherham Archives & Local Studies Service
Rotherham Advertiser 2/1/1965
Kellys Directory 1970, 1971

Harrison Proctor
Rotherham Archives & Local Studies Service
Information Rotherham Advertiser 5/12/1980
Goad Maps 1984,2001,2002

Photograph
Philip H J Smedley

Wellgate Post Office
Information
Rotherham Archives & Local Studies Service
Hill Norman Postal History of Rotherham & District ref 942.741/383

Photograph
Rotherham Family History Society
Wellgate 1962 Colin Leonard Collection

Francis Dunford, Draper 121 Wellgate
Information
Rotherham Archives & Local Studies Service
Kellys Directories

Photographs
Don Wainman

Fred Elliott, House Furnishers
Information
Mrs Elliott, Mrs Diane Shaw
Rotherham Archives & Local Studies Service
Rotherham Express 16/7/1938

Photograph [pt] Rotherham Family History Society
Elliotts Colin Leonard Collection 1964

Fred Elliott 1940, Rolls Royce Mrs Diane Shaw

Bygone Hairdressers
Information
Rotherham Archives & Local Studies Service
Kellys Directories, Goad Maps 1995, 1998
HURC Monday Club

Photographs
Rotherham Family History Society
Les Blaireaux Colin Leonard Collection 1961
Ivy Payne [pt] Colin Leonard 1964

178 Wellgate
Information & **Photograph**
Roger & Maureen Longdin

Deans Electrical
Rotherham Archives & Local Studies Service
Rotherham Advertiser 15/10/1993
Information
Mrs Shirley Cutts

R H Thickett Butcher
Information
Mr John Thickett , Mr George Humphrey
Rotherham Archives & Local Studies Service
Kellys Directories 1898,1901,1908,1916,1939,1974.

Photograph Rotherham Family History Society,
Cleaver Buildings Colin Leonard Collection 1964

F L Smith
Information
Mrs Elaine Secluna
Rotherham Archives & Local Studies Service
Kellys Directories 1936, 1948, 1962, 1963.

Bob Hague Newsagent
Rotherham Archives & Local Studies Service
Rotherham Annual 1959
Rotherham Advertiser 7/2/1975

Photograph ref 00185 1939 photographer unknown

Richardson's Newsagent
Rotherham Archives & Local Studies Service
Rotherham Advertiser 16/10/1987,
Advertisement 5/12/1980

Norman Speight Purveyors of Tripe
Information
Mrs Speight
Rotherham Archives & Local Studies Service
Rotherham Advertiser 10/10/1980, 15/7/1994.

A Russell Butcher
Information
Mrs Carol Smout
Mrs Angela Sorsby

Photograph
Daily Independent
Press Cuttings & Olympic Medal Mrs Carol Smout

Stockdales Fruiterers
Information
Mrs Carol Burton

Photograph
Frank Stockdale 1935
Mrs Carol Burton

Ernest Giles
Information
Mrs Margaret Rayner.

Photograph
Rotherham Archives & Local Studies Service
Lyons Ice Cream 00184 Photographer unknown

E C Sayers
Information
Rotherham Archives & Local Studies Service
Rotherham Advertiser 5/6/1998

Advertisements -
(Rotherham Archives & Local Studies Service).
Rotherham Advertiser [unless otherwise specified]
Allied Facilities 6/9/1952,

Pearsons Rotherham Annual 1953
Appleby & Miles 28/7/1962, Courtney's 19/11/1971,
W. Kaybee 19/11/1971
Wilkes, 19/11/1971, Audrey Dakin 5/12/11980, Wil-Be-Fort 25/1/1964,
The Spinning Wheel Wool Co 6/9/1952, Lennox Sewing Machines 19/11/1971.

C. Denham 6/9/1952,

David Price 6/9/1952, O& J Waters 8/2/1964,
Wilfred Hill 28/10/1950. J W Sellars 6/3/1965

HHB Sugg Ltd 19/11/1971, 21/7/1962

Edwin Clover & Sons 6/9/1952,

Orly Travel Ltd 18/1/1964

Holgans 15/2/1964 + 27/7/1963

Mary Reaney 5/12/1980,

Ivy Payne 6/9/1952
Patricia Kellett Rotherham Annual 1953

Deans Electrical 19/11/1971

F L Smith, 6/9/1952

Richardson's Newsagent 5/12/1980

Ye Old Gate Café 6/9/1952, Health food store 19/11/1971
Norman Speight 6/9/1952
Rickshaw Restaurant 14/4/1962, Denhams Tea Rooms 25/1/2002

Central Motor Works 29/3/1958, 21/3/1925,
EC Sayers & Co Ltd 6/3/1965, 6/9/1952,
Colin Bucknall 2/5/1964, Ball & Waite 13/7/1935

Dalkins 19/1/1971, 6/9/1952

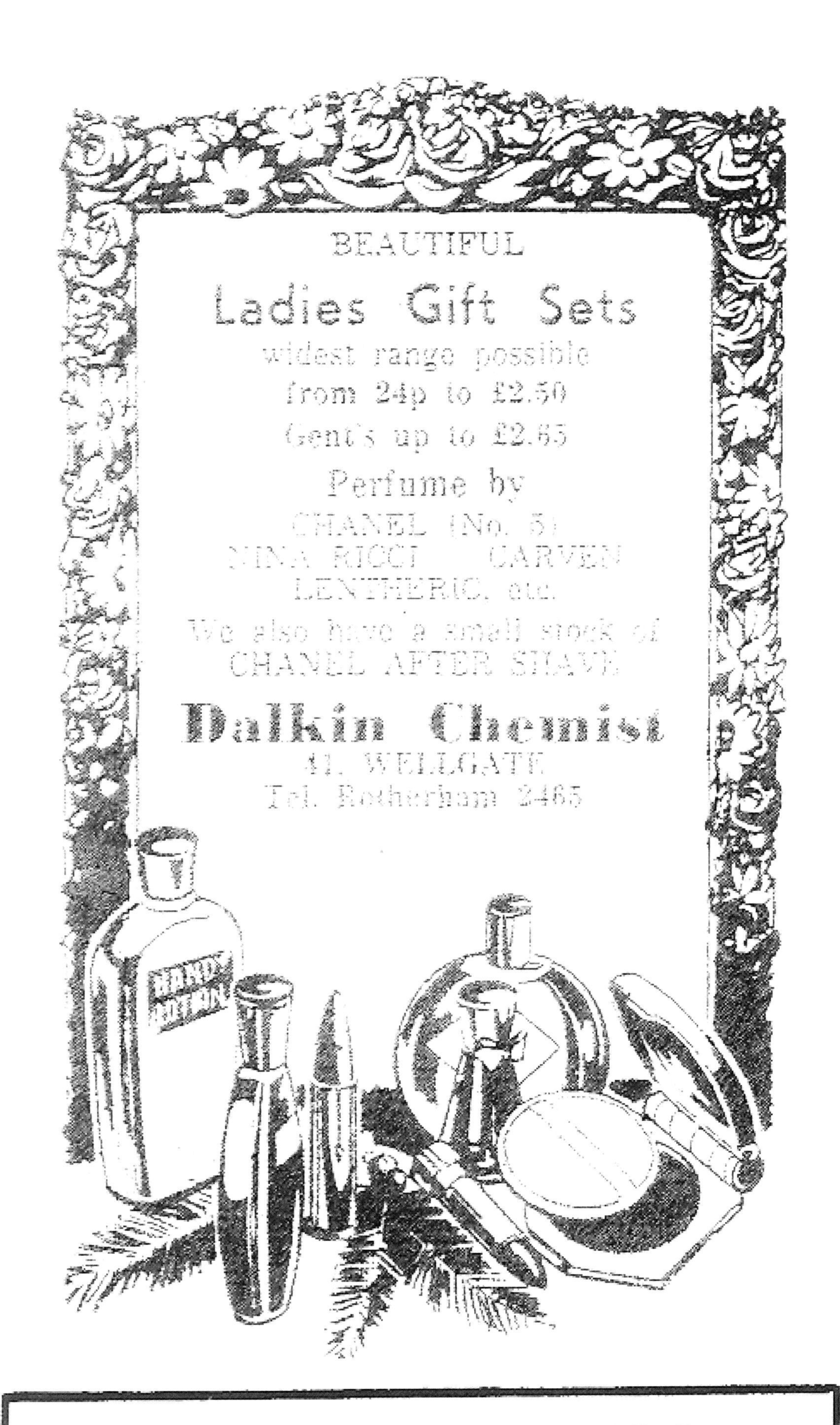
BEAUTIFUL
Ladies Gift Sets
widest range possible
from 24p to £2.50
Gent's up to £2.65
Perfume by
CHANEL (No. 5)
NINA RICCI CARVEN
LENTHERIC, etc.
We also have a small stock of
CHANEL AFTER SHAVE
Dalkin Chemist
41, WELLGATE
Tel. Rotherham 2465

Chapter 7

Wellgate Public Houses

Cleaver Inn 10 Wellgate

Present building erected 1926
Earliest known date 1792

Licensees	
1822-1824	William Eaton
1885-1889	Samuel Earnshaw
1922-1930	Henry E Flintham

RFHS Colin Leonard **Cleaver Inn**

The Cleaver Inn, one of the oldest public houses in Rotherham has undergone name changes in recent years to Magintys, Tut 'n' Shive back to Cleaver Inn and then No 10 and is now currently closed.

In 1843 two gentlemen named Cobden and Bright visited Rotherham to speak about 'The Corn Law Question'. This took place at the Cleaver Inn in the farmer's dining room 'amid the fumes of Church Wardens'.

Around the same period guests at the Crown Hotel were divided into the House of Lords who dined upstairs and the House of Commons who dined downstairs. The farmers who were a lower class were 'put up' at the Cleaver Inn and 'lower still' guests, stayed at the Bluebell and Wheatsheaf.

In 1926 the Cleaver Inn was replaced by a more modern building reflecting the requirements of the day. A brick fireplace and rafted ceiling were included to give an old world feeling to the new Inn. Also planned was a spacious courtyard and garage. The Inn had an entrance onto Wellgate in addition to the public bar entrance under the old archway and the frontage of the building contained a sales-shop with offices above.

The Hare and Hounds 52 Wellgate

Earliest Date 1841

Licensees
1841-1854 George Wright
1886-1901 James V Jepson
1906-1926 William H Wragg

The Hare and Hounds Public house dates back to 1841.

Rotherham Old Brewery Co made an application in 1900 to make certain alterations plus the addition of a new kitchen, small cellar and cellar kitchen.

In 1938 Wellgate Improvement plans meant the demolition of the Hare & Hounds, the Oddfellows Arms and other adjacent properties.

Later that year Messrs Bentleys Brewery proposed the demolition of the Hare and Hounds and the rebuilding of a new three-storey public house conforming to the new Wellgate Improvement line.

Although the Oddfellows Arms was demolished the intervention of World War Two prevented the scheme going ahead.

Further plans in 1949 for demolition and rebuilding of the public house did not take place thus saving this original Inn.

Trade in 1959 was recorded as 5 x 36 barrels and 80 dozen bottles per week.

In 1901 the Rotherham Advertiser reported 76 licensed victuallers and 66 beerhouse keepers in the borough in addition to 48 shopkeepers licensed to sell beer and 19 persons licensed to sell wines & spirits. With a population of 54,348 the ratio was one licensed house to every 260 persons. Now closed.

The Mail Coach Inn 14 Wellgate

Earliest Date 1825

Licensees

1825-1840	Emmanuel Jarvis
1898-1905	W Flintham
1917-1925	James Gibson

Ref 14752 **1911 - 1915**

For travellers journeying by coach the Inns were an essential part of the transport system. They provided a resting place for both traveller and horses at regular intervals along the route. Some Inns combined both coaching and carrying facilities and the Inn yards were used for loading and unloading goods. The earliest record of The Mail Coach Inn is 1825 when Emmanuel Jarvis was landlord. Prior to this the Inn was known as The Saddle kept by G A Vause.

Sheffield & Rotherham Directory 1841 records that Gigs and saddle horses were let at the Mail Coach Inn, Wellgate.

In 1880 an advertisement in the Rotherham Advertiser announced the auction of the 'old established Free Licensed public house or Inn known as the Mail Coach, Wellgate'.

Details of the premises were given:

The house contained front and bar parlours, tap room, snug and kitchen on the ground floor and one large and three smaller bedrooms. Out-premises consisted of a yard, large clubroom, stabling for eighteen horses and piggery. The Inn was centrally situated and had a good reputation and connection as a Market House.

Farmer's carts and carrier carts laden with produce gathered outside the Mail Coach and Cleaver Inn on a Friday night providing a wholesale market.**[ch 4]** In 1906 an application was made to make additions and alterations to the Inn, and the yard to be paved in stone cobbles for Whitworth Son & Nephew Ltd, Wath on Dearne.

What remained of the stables behind the Mail Coach were deemed unsafe and demolished in 2010.

The Masons Arms 159 Wellgate

Earliest Date 1825

Licensees

1825-1831	John Mellor
1886-1906	George H Collins
1929-1954	J E Tattershall

RFHS **The Masons Arms**

The Masons Arms dates back to 1825 when John Mellor was licensee. Prior to this the Masons was a private house occupied by Johnny Dobb. The original Masons Arms was demolished in the late 1880's and it is thought a new Inn was built more or less on the same site.

From 1929-1954 the licensee was John Tattershall and in 1932 he placed an advertisement in the Rotherham Advertiser:

In 1959 the Licensing Justices recorded the landlord was running a good house and selling 7 x 36 barrels and 70-80 dozen bottles per week.

In 1962 a club opened in the Masons Arms known as the 'Taveners Folk Group' co-founded by Stan Crowther. **[chapter 5]** Now closed.

The Oddfellows Arms 44 Wellgate

Earliest Date 1833
Closed 1938

Licensees

1833-1866	Martha Harris
1884-1889	J Burgoyne
1917-1925	Sarah Tyers

Ref 00187 The Oddfellows Arms

The Oddfellows Arms, situated at 44 Wellgate was previously known as the Moulders Arms.

The beerhouse dated back to 1833 when Martha Harris was licensee.

In 1900 Mappins Brewery submitted an application to make additions to the premises.

Another application was made in 1934 for an extension to the licensed premises. There was a covered archway leading to a yard with two stables. The new application was designed to alter the back of the building and demolish the stables leaving an open yard.

In March 1938 the Rotherham Advertiser reported that the Rotherham Licensing Bench had refused to renew the license of the beerhouse. The reasons given were that the trade of the public house amounted to three and a half barrels per week and there were several other licensed premises in the locality.

After closure Rotherham Corporation acquired the premises and the Oddfellows Arms were demolished to prepare for the Wellgate Improvement plans to widen the road. This scheme did not take place and the site now forms the small car park next to the Hare and Hounds.

The William IV

A small beerhouse thought to be located at 15 Wellgate on the corner of Old Hill and Wellgate. Due to rebuilding over the years the Old Hill signage has long since gone. In 1833 the beerhouse was kept by William Pearson, its name disappearing by 1837.

In 1872 it was listed as a licensed house under John Schofield but had changed to a shoe-makers shop in 1881. The building eventually became a gentleman's hairdressers and by 1974 had been demolished.

The Pack Horse Inn 1 Wellgate/ 2 Doncaster Gate

Earliest known Date 1792
Closed 1904

Licensees 1814-1824 Ann Babb
1825-1841 William Babb
1897-1904 Robert Matley

The Pack Horse Inn situated at the junction of Wellgate and Doncaster Gate probably dated back to the late eighteenth century. William Babb was licensee from 1825-1841 following on from Ann Babb. Being a religious man he was well known in the town for his 'Bible roasting' activities.

Ref 00227 **The Pack Horse Inn 1898-1902**

In 1893 the property was acquired by Rotherham Corporation for the purpose of street improvements. Nine years later in 1902 the premises were advertised for sale including a yard and stabling for twelve horses.

The Inn was purchased by William Stones Ltd subject to the Licensing Justices approva l for the re building plans. This was not forthcoming.

In 1903 William Wing purchased the property and passed ownership to the Old Albion Brewery who intended to demolish the existing building and build a new public house.

Plans for a four storey Hotel to be built on the site of the Old Pack Horse Inn containing twenty-two bedrooms with accommodation for commercial travellers and hotel guests. The ground floor would have a smoking room, billiard room and spacious hall and the first floor a large dining room and suite of rooms. Stabling accommodation to be provided.

Application was made at the licensing sessions in February 1904 for renewal of the licence but various objections were made including one from the Temperance Movement and the licence was refused. In July 1904 a letter to the Town Clerk of Rotherham on behalf of the Old Albion Brewery expressed dissatisfaction with their treatment regarding refusal of the licence and new building plans. It was suggested that the Corporation should take back the properties.

The Pack Horse Inn was subsequently sold for shopping re development in 1906. [chapter 6]

The Three Tuns 142 Wellgate

Earliest Date 1822 - Closed 1938

Licensees

1822	Thomas Badger
1922-1930	Fred Pickersgill

Pauline & Michael Bentley Collection **The Three Tuns 1905**

The Three Tuns was situated at the junction of Hollowgate and Wellgate and dated from 1822 when Thomas Badger was licensee. It was the original meeting place of the Oddfellows lodge established in 1864.

The Three Tuns had an Angling Association and in August 1882 their annual match was held at Misterton. Twenty six competitors took part and eighteen caught fish. Six prizes were awarded for the largest fish 1st, 1 lb 2 1/2 oz to 6th 5oz.

In 1938 objections were made to the renewal of the license for the Three Tuns. The front entrance was below ground level and the passage badly lit, the best room held 32 persons but was obscured from the bar and the taproom could not be supervised from the bar. There was poor lighting in the kitchen and the upstairs accommodation was damp and in need of repair.

The trade was about five to six barrels and twenty dozen bottles per week. The Bentley Trustees opposed the closure saying that there was ample room for rebuilding. The magistrates decided against the trustees and The Three Tuns closed in 1938 accommodating road junction improvements.

RFHS **The Three Tuns**

The Rose and Crown 11 Quarry Hill

Earliest known date 1833
Closed 1907

Licensees

1833-1841	Henry Ross
1873-1881	Job Athey
1905-1907	William G Foster

Listed as a Beerhouse and known as the Reform Tavern in 1833 it had changed its name to the Rose and Crown by 1845 and was known to regulars as 'The Snug'.

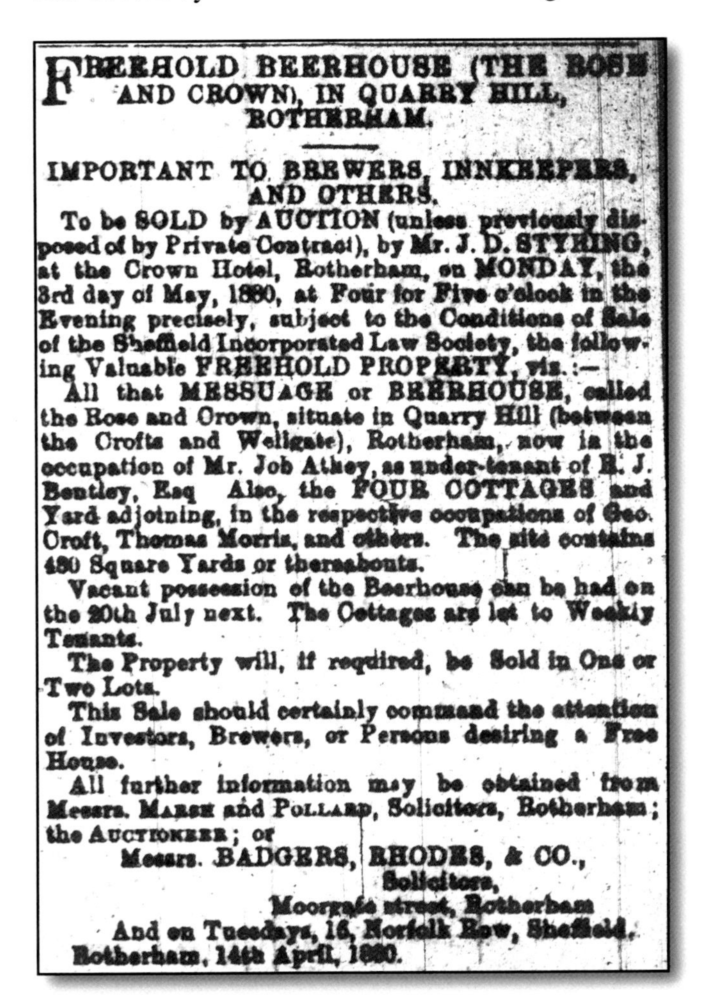

FREEHOLD BEERHOUSE (THE ROSE AND CROWN), IN QUARRY HILL, ROTHERHAM.

IMPORTANT TO BREWERS, INNKEEPERS, AND OTHERS.

To be SOLD by AUCTION (unless previously disposed of by Private Contract), by Mr. J. D. STYRING, at the Crown Hotel, Rotherham, on MONDAY, the 3rd day of May, 1880, at Four for Five o'clock in the Evening precisely, subject to the Conditions of Sale of the Sheffield Incorporated Law Society, the following Valuable FREEHOLD PROPERTY, viz.:—

All that MESSUAGE or BEERHOUSE, called the Rose and Crown, situate in Quarry Hill (between the Crofts and Wellgate), Rotherham, now in the occupation of Mr. Job Athey, as under-tenant of R. J. Bentley, Esq Also, the FOUR COTTAGES and Yard adjoining, in the respective occupations of Geo. Croft, Thomas Morris, and others. The site contains 480 Square Yards or thereabouts.

Vacant possession of the Beerhouse can be had on the 20th July next. The Cottages are let to Weekly Tenants.

The Property will, if required, be Sold in One or Two Lots.

This Sale should certainly command the attention of Investors, Brewers, or Persons desiring a Free House.

All further information may be obtained from Messrs. MARSH and POLLARD, Solicitors, Rotherham; the AUCTIONEER; or

Messrs. BADGERS, RHODES, & CO., Solicitors, Moorgate street, Rotherham

And on Tuesdays, 16, Norfolk Row, Sheffield.

Rotherham, 14th April, 1880.

In May 1880 the Rotherham Advertiser advertised a notice to auction the Rose and Crown and four cottages situated in Quarry Hill.

Gummer recorded that the 'Monday Cattle Market was crowded and frequently overflowed into Mansfield Road, and the Rose and Crown in Quarry Hill did a roaring trade at market times'.

After closure in 1907 the Rose and Crown became a lodging house and was run by Mrs Sarah Marriott from 1922 until approximately 1950.

The property was acquired by Vere's Bakery and demolished in 1952 to enable further expansion of their business.

A number of other beerhouses on Wellgate are recorded in the directories of the time most of which do not have a precise location:

George and Dragon a beerhouse kept by William Clark in 1833.

The Harrow recorded in 1822 when Thomas Steer was Innkeeper

The Saddle a beerhouse in 1822 kept by GA Vause later to become The Mailcoach

Speed the Plough a beerhouse in 1833 kept by Anne Challenge

Refs
Mr Jim Clark - Information on all the Public Houses and Beerhouses in Wellgate
Satterthwaite Paul Rotherham Town Public Houses 1820-1990
Jennings Paul 'The Local' A History of the English Pub 2011 647/954 2

Rotherham Archives & Local Studies Service
Various Trade Directories-
History Directory & Gazeteer of the County of York 1822/1823. Vol 1 West Riding- Baines ref 942/74 ST
Directory of Sheffield etc 1825 – R Gell Ref 942/74-SHE ST
History & Directory of Sheffield 1833- White Ref 942/74 SHE ST
History & Directory of Sheffield 1837 William White Ref 942/74 SHE ST
Sheffield & Rotherham Directory H A & T Rodgers Ref 942/74 SHE ST
Sheffield & Rotherham etc 1841 White Ref 942/74 SHE ST
Directory of Sheffield etc 1856 William White Ref 942/74 SHE ST
General Directory of Sheffield 1860 Ref 942/74 SHE ST
General Directory & Topography of the Borough of Sheffield & 12 Miles Around including Rotherham 10th edition 1864 White Ref 942/74 SHE ST
Directory of Sheffield White 1872 ref 942/74 SHE ST

Additional Information
The Cleaver Inn
Rotherham Archives & Local Studies Service
Rotherham Advertiser 22/5/1926
Reminiscences of Rotherham & District published 1891- A series of letters to Rotherham Advertiser reminiscing about the 1830's & 1840's
Ivanhoe Review Vol 2 page 21 1899
Kellys Directories 1885, 1889, 1922, 1930

The Hare & Hounds
Rotherham Archives & Local Studies Service
Kellys Directories 1901, 1906, 1926
Building Regulations Plans 1897-1948
16/8/1900 – ref 3278, 17/6/1938 ref 8707.
Rotherham Advertiser 31/8/1901

The Mail Coach
Jennings Paul The History of the English Pub
Rotherham Archives & Local Studies Service
Rotherham Advertiser 17/1/1880, 6/9/1952
Building Regulations 1897-1948
Sheffield & Rotherham directory1841 H A &T Rodgers ref 942/74 SHE.ST
Kellys Directories 1898, 1905, 1917, 1925.
Mr Barry Worrall current Landlord Mail Coach Inn

The Masons Arms
Rotherham Archives & Local Studies Service
Reminiscences of Rotherham & District 1891 from a series of letters about the 1830's-1840's. ref 942/741
Kellys Directories 1906, 1925
Stan Crowther [chapter 5 refs]
Advertisement
Rotherham Advertiser 19/11/1932.

The Oddfellows Arms
Rotherham Archives & Local Studies Service
Building Regulations Plans 1897-1948
1900- Ref 061&Bld 3261, 1934 Ref 061-Bld 6972
Rotherham Advertiser 5/3/1938 page 9
Kellys Directories 1925

William 1V 1833 Whites Directory
1872 Whites Directory of Sheffield
1881, 1973, 1974 Kellys Directories

The Pack Horse Inn
Information
Mr Jim Clark, Licensing Sessions 1904, letter to Town Clerk
Hawkridge Ian & Peter - A Pub Crawl Through History 2010
Rotherham Archives & Local Studies Service
Rotherham Advertiser 20/2/1904, 2/7/1904
Kellys Directories 1897-1904

The Three Tuns
Rotherham Archives & Local Studies Service
Rotherham Advertiser 12/8/1882, 5/3/1938
Kellys Directories 1922, 1930

Photographs

RHFS
Cleaver Inn [pt photo] Colin Leonard
The Masons Arms
The Three Tuns

Rotherham Archives & Local Studies Service
Mail Coach Inn ref 14752 photographer unknown
Oddfellows Arms ref 00187 photographer unknown
Pack Horse Inn ref 00227 photographer unknown
New proposed Pack Horse Inn Rotherham Advertiser 20/2/1904

Pauline & Michael Bentley Collection
The Three Tuns 1905

Ralph Jackson
Hare & Hounds

The Rose & Crown
Rotherham Archives & Local Studies Service
White Archive ref book 89-F/B/4/4-
Old deeds relating to ownership of the land transcribed for Dorothy Greene by Mr S A Carr 1952
Kellys Directories 1881, 1883, 1907, 1922, 1949
Licensing Registers 1869-1879
Business Directory Sheffield & Rotherham 1862
Gummer G Reminiscences of Rotherham 1927
Rotherham Advertiser Advertisement 24/4/ 1880

George and Dragon 1833 Whites Directory
The Harrow 1822 Baines Directory
The Saddle 1822 Baines Directory
Speed the Plough 1833 Whites Directory

Chapter 8

Wellgate Occupants
Their Trade and Professions 1862

William Alsop	Grocer	Wellgate
Alfred Atkinson	Post Office Clerk	57 Wellgate
Matthew Bairstow	Shopkeeper	87 Wellgate
Mary Bairstow	Milliner	87 Wellgate
Jasper Beckett	Grocer	Wellgate
Miss Ann Birkett		Yard 3 Wellgate
John Bottomley	Boot & Shoemaker	15 Wellgate
John Bower	Gardener & Seedsman	80 Wellgate
Thomas Bower	Asphalt Road Maker	Wellgate
William Butterfield	Clerk	68 Wellgate
William Eyre Buxton	Victualler - Mail Coach	Wellgate
Ruth Cawood	Straw Bonnet Maker	54 Wellgate
William Cook	Shopkeeper	69 Wellgate
Rupert Cooke	Forman Millwright	64 Wellgate
Thomas Cox	Cabinet Maker & Upholsterer	3 Wellgate
Thomas Darwent	Sadler	7 Wellgate
Thomas Dent		1 Radley Row Wellgate
John Flute	Keeper of Model Lodging House	Wellgate
Jarvis Guest	Victualler - Masons Arms	103 Wellgate
John Hale	Draper & Marine Store Dealer	22 Wellgate
George Hall	Beerhouse Keeper	Wellgate
George Hargreave	Clothes Dealer	33 Wellgate
Martha Harris	Beerhousekeeper	42 Wellgate
Moses Harris	Plasterer & Dealer in Cement	53 Wellgate
John Haukrigg	Victualler - Pack Horse	Wellgate
Samuel Hird	Shopkeeper	30 Wellgate
Hugh Hoyland	Accountant, Collector & Agent to Clerical Medical & General Life Office [Home Broom Villa Whiston]	Wellgate
Hudson & Sutton	Agent to Consolidated Life & Loan Assurance Co & Victoria Benefit Society	4 Wellgate
William Hudson	Shopkeeper	133 Wellgate
William Hudson	Cabinet Maker & Furniture Broker	4&5 Wellgate
William Hutton	Shopkeeper	34 Wellgate
Oliver Cromwell James	Basket Maker	39 Wellgate
Emmanuel & Thomas Jarvis	Hay & Straw Dealer	84 Wellgate
Hiram Jephson	Hat Cleaner	28 Wellgate
Mrs Jephson	Straw Bonnet Maker	28 Wellgate
Mary Kay	Dressmaker	Wellgate
John Kenning	Shopkeeper & Newsagent	31 Wellgate
George Kent	Shopkeeper	Wellgate
Richard Laycock	Victualler - Three Tuns	Wellgate
Thomas Lent	Draper	Wellgate
George Mellor	Postman	36 Wellgate
William Mellor	Shopkeeper	26 Wellgate
James Clifford Morgan	Commercial Traveller	Wellgate
Jas Goodrick Needham	Watch & Clockmaker	1 Wellgate
John Needham	Cab Proprietor	1 Wellgate
Edward Norman	Chemist, Druggist & Soda Water Manufacturer	44 Wellgate
Miss Emma Norman		1 Wellgate House
John Oxley	Greengrocer	5 Wellgate
Edward Parry	Agent	105 Wellgate
Thomas Pearson	Tailor	101 Wellgate
Jacob Rawson	Greengrocer	18 Wellgate
William Richardson	Piano-forte Tuner	61 Wellgate
Benjamin Robinson	MD & General Practitioner	6 Wellgate
George Rodgers	Shoemaker	95 Wellgate
Ann Sharp	Shopkeeper	11 Wellgate

Joseph Slack	Greengrocer	13 Wellgate
Henry Ephram Slawson	Bricklayer & Builder	69 Wellgate
William Smith	Nail Manufacturer	107 Wellgate
Henry Spurr	Shopkeeper & Plasterer	17 Wellgate
William Sutton	Insurance Agent [Hudson & Son]	Wellgate
Miss Sarah Swain		Poplar Cottage, Wellgate
Edward Tomlinson	Grocer	19 Wellgate
George Walker	Slater	37 Wellgate
Henry Walker	Slater & Shopkeeper	27 Wellgate
Hannah Ward	Greengrocer	41 Wellgate
Samuel Watson	Nail Manufacturer	Yard 76 Wellgate
Joseph Wells	Dyer	46 Wellgate
William Wells		59 Wellgate
John Whitaker	Victualler – Cleaver	10 Wellgate
Thomas Whitaker	Raft & Timber Dealer & Joiner	Wellgate [Home Herringthorpe]
Whittington Brothers	Black Shoeing Smiths	College Street & Wellgate
George Williams	Herbalist	Yard 53 Wellgate
John Ebenezer William	Manufacturing Chemist	Wellgate [Home Wellgate House]
Henry Womak	Accountant & Co	93 Wellgate [Home Broom Cottage Whiston]
Mary Woolhouse	Shopkeeper	20 Wellgate
George Wragg	Victualler – Hare & Hounds	Wellgate
Humphrey Wright	Auctioneer & Cabinet Maker	Wellgate
Mr HS Wright RACM	Professor of Music	9 Wellgate
Charles Yates	Grocer	12 Wellgate
Young Mens Christian Association		Wellgate

Trades and Professions Wellgate 1862

Accountants & Collectors

Hugh Hoyland	Wellgate
Henry Womak	93 Wellgate

Asphalter

Thomas Bower	101 Wellgate

Auctioneers

Humphrey Wright	Wellgate

Basket Maker

Oliver C James	39 Wellgate

Boot & Shoemakers

John Bottomley	15 Wellgate
George Rodgers	95 Wellgate

Cabinet Makers

Thomas Cox	3 Wellgate
William Hudson	Wellgate
Humphrey Wright	Wellgate

Chemist & Druggists

Edward Norman	44 Wellgate

Chemists
[Manufacturing]

John Ebenezer Williams	Wellgate

Dyer

Joseph Wells	46 Wellgate

Fire & Life Officers

Hugh Hoyland Clerical, Medical & General	Wellgate
Hutton & Sutton Consolidated Life & Loan & Victoria Benefit	4 Wellgate

Furniture Broker

Thomas Cox	3 Wellgate

Gardeners [*Greengrocers only]

John Bower	80 Wellgate
*John Oxley	56 Wellgate
*Jacob Rawson	18 Wellgate
*Joseph Slack	13 Wellgate
*Hannah Ward	41 Wellgate

Grocers & Tea Dealers
[*Provisions Dealers]

William Alsop	Wellgate
Jasper Beckett	Wellgate
*Edward Tomlinson	19 Wellgate
*Charles Yates	12 Wellgate

Hatters

Hiram Jephson [Cleaner]	28 Wellgate

Hay & Straw Dealers

Emmanuel Jarvis	84 Wellgate
Thomas Jarvis	84 Wellgate

Herbalist

George Williams	5 Wellgate

Horse & Gig Letters
[* & Cab Proprietor]

*John Needham	1 Wellgate

Hotels, Inns & Taverns

John Whitaker – Cleaver	10 Wellgate
George Wragg – Hare & Hounds	Wellgate
William Eyre Buxton - Mail Coach	14 Wellgate
Jarvis Guest - Masons Arms	103Wellgate
John Haukrigg - Pack Horse	Wellgate
Richard Laycock - - Three Tuns	Wellgate

Beerhouses

George Hall	Wellgate
Martha Harris	42 Wellgate

Joiners & Builders

Thomas Whitaker	Wellgate

Land & Estate Agents

Hugh Hoyland	Wellgate

Linen & Woollen Drapers

John Hale	22 Wellgate
Thomas Lent	21 Wellgate

Milliners & Dressmakers
[*Straw Bonnet Makers]

Elizabeth Dent — Radley Row
*Mary Jephson — 28 Wellgate
Mary Kay — Wellgate

Music Professors

Mr H S Wright RACM — 9 Wellgate

Nail Makers

William Smith — 107 Wellgate
Samuel Watson Yard — 76 Wellgate

Newsagents

John Kenny — 31 Wellgate

Physicians *Surgeons

***Benjamin Robinson** — 6 Wellgate

Piano-Forte Tuner

William Richardson — 61 Wellgate

Plasterers

Henry Spurr — 17 Wellgate

Rag & Bone Dealers

John Hale — 22 Wellgate

Saddlers & Harness Makers

Thomas Darwent — 7 Wellgate

Shopkeepers

Wiliam Cook — 69 Wellgate
Samuel Hird — 30 Wellgate
William Hudson — 133 Wellgate
William Hutton — 34 Wellgate
John Kenning — 31 Wellgate
George Kent — Wellgate
William Mellor — 26 Wellgate
Ann Sharp — 11 Wellgate
Henry Spurr — 17 Wellgate
Henry Walke — 27 Wellgate
Mary Woolhouse — 20 Wellgate

Slaters

Henry Walker — 27 Wellgate

Soda Water & Manufacturers

Edward Norman — 44 Wellgate

Refs Drakes Directory 1862

Stone Mason, Bricklayer
& Builders

Ephraim Slawson — 69 Wellgate

Straw Bonnet Maker

Ruth Cawood — 54 Wellgate
Mary Jephson — 28 Wellgate

Surgeons

Benjamin Robinson — 6 Wellgate

Taylors

Thomas Dent — 1 Radley Row Wellgate
Thomas Pearson — 101 Wellgate

Timber & Slate Merchants

Thomas Whitaker — Wellgate

Watchmaker

James Goodrick Needham — 1 Wellgate

Acknowledgements
Rotherham Metropolitan Borough Council, Archives & Local Studies Service.
Lisa Broadest, Manager, Heritage Services, for her kind permission to use Archive material, her staff Julie and Pat for their patience & help throughout this project and Tim Brannan for his invaluable assistance.

With grateful thanks to the following:
Mr Doug Melloy, Editor, Rotherham Advertiser, for permission to use information & advertisements. Rotherham Family History Society, South Yorkshire Transport Museum and Rotherham Archaeological Society.
Philip H J Smedley, Jim Clark, Paul Fox, CC Hall, Mrs M Wilson, Mrs M Houghton,
Ian Jones, John Ridsdale, Paul Nicholson, Clare Watts, Joan Pybus, Mark Edgell,
David & John Clennell, Mrs M Openshaw[nee Leadbeater,] Richard Allen,
Andrew Cunningham, Pauline & Michael Bentley, Rev P Edwards, CC Souter,
Craig Bannister, Members of Ebenezer Wesleyan Reform Church,
John Hargreaves, JS Crowther, David Taylor, Barbara Littlewood, George Humphrey,
John Thickett, Pippa Harder, D Clover, P Thackray, Elaine Secluna, Christine Wilson,
Mrs Speight, Carol Smout, Angela Sorsby,D Blomfield, U Lambert, Carol Burton,
S Morrison, Mrs Elliott, Diane Shaw, Janet Worrall, D Wainman, P Satterthwaite,
Ian & Peter Hawkridge, D Hodgkinson, K Marshall, Howard Johnson, P Thornborrow,
P & M Findlater, Stuart Lister, HURC Monday Club, Mrs D Nicholls Mrs K Taylor, Maureen & Roger Longdin,
K Holdsworth, D Wainman, Michael Hague, Tony Bryan, MA Croft, W Mapplebeck
Brian & Shirley Cutts, Dr GB Peckitt, Tony Bartholomew, Janette & Paul Haigh.

Bibliography

Guest John	Historic Notices of Rotherham 1879
Smith Howard	A History of Rotherham's Roads & Transport 1992
Hall CC	Rotherham & District Transport Volumes 1, 2, & 3 1996/1998/1999.
Gummer G	Reminiscences of Rotherham 1927
	The Feoffees of The Common Lands of Rotherham
	Yorkshire Water Newspaper April 1978 edition 19
Hill Norman	Postal History of Rotherham & District 1960
Cockburn J	Rotherham Lawyers During 350 Years 1932
Cater P M	A Short History of Education in the County Borough of Rotherham 1871 - 1974
Beggs Thomas	Sketch of the Life & Labours of Mr Alderman John Guest FSA 1881
Young Arthur	Six Months Tour 1769
Morris E	'Eastwood View' 1971
Munford AP	Victorian Rotherham 1989, A History of Rotherham 2000, Rotherham Past & Present 2001.
Blazeby W Rev	Rotherham Old Meeting House & Its Ministers1906
	Drakes Directory 1862
Crowder Freda & Greene Dorothy	Rotherham Its History, Church & Chapel 1971
Crowther Stan	'One Thing After Another' 2005
Worrall Janet	Moorgate Cemetery, A Stroll Around Victorian Rotherham
Satterthwaite Paul	Rotherham Town Public Houses 1991
Jennings Paul	'The Local' A History of the English Pub 2011
Hawkridge Ian & Peter	A Pub Crawl through History 2010
Blomfield D	Extract of Kew Past 1994
Lambert U Appendix	The Barn Church of St Philip The Apostle & All Saints 1936
Brand E	Rotherham Parish Church One Thousand Years 937-1937
	Advertisement Moorhouse & Co.

Rotherham Archives & Local Studies Service:

Various Directories & Archive Catalogues as listed
Licensing Registers 1869-1879
Rotherham Annuals
Listed Buildings Book
Rotherham Corporation Waterworks: The History of Rotherham's Water Supplies 1971
Lee William Report to the General Board of Health 1851
Mansergh James Report on Sewage 25th May 1881
Bockley Agnes & Callear Veronica Wellgate Old Hall
Methodist Press Cuttings Books 1 & 2
Rotherham Circuit Wellgate Historical Documents 1859-1903
Pew Rental 1859-1870
Wellgate Primitive Methodist Church hand written book 1930
Coward PB Press Cuttings
Wellgate School Log Books 1921-1951, 1951-1963
Ivanhoe Review Vol 1 No 6 1898, Vol 2 1899
Souvenir Grand Rainbow Bazaar 1913
Reminiscences of Rotherham & District 1891
Buildings Regulations Plans 1897-1948
Whittington & Whittington Blacksmiths 1859
Rotherham Hospital Pamphlets [Doncaster Gate]

The Rotherham Amateur Repertory Company Information
James Jenkin Day Book 1898-1902
Crowther J S Press Cuttings

Rotherham Advertiser
Press Cuttings & Advertisements

Rotherham Star & Express
Press Cuttings as listed

Maps
Rotherham Archives & Local Studies Service
Early Rotherham 1925 Dorothy Greene
Ordnance Survey Maps 1888 & 1901

Illustrations Acknowledgement
Every effort has been made to contact or trace copyright holders. The Publishers will be glad to make good any errors or omissions brought to our attention in future editions. We are grateful to the following for permission to reproduce illustrative material.
Rotherham Archives & Local Studies Service, Rotherham Family History Society [RFHS],
Rotherham Advertiser, Pauline & Michael Bentley, Barbara Littlewood, Philip HJ Smedley, M Wilson, D Hodgkinson, Paul Nicholson, Clare Watts, David & John Clennell, Paul Fox, J Reader, S L Smith,
H Johnson, C C Souter, John Hargreaves, J S Crowther, D Clover, P Thackray, Carol Smout,
Carol Burton, Diane Shaw, Maureen & Roger Longdin, Don Wainman, P & J Haigh, MA Croft,
Dr GB Peckitt, W Mapplebeck, Joan & Philip Graham, Ralph Jackson.

Photographs
Rotherham Archives & Local Studies Service [photos denoted by reference number]
Mainly unknown photographers with the exception of:
Van Allans 1907 ref 11024 Rotherham Advertiser LMA
Wellgate 1926-1935 ref 00175 AFS
Vere's Bakery 1937 ref 05611 Sheffield Telegraph LMA
Wellgate School Programme 1886
PMC x 2 Souvenir Grand Rainbow Bazaar 1913

Rotherham Family History Society [RFHS]
Collections of Colin Leonard & George Bentley, J E Twible

The Paul Fox Collection
J Reader Trams up Wellgate
E L Scrivens Passing Loop 1908-1924
S L Smith Trolley Bus 52 1928
Advertisement Tramway Supplies

Pauline & Michael Bentley Collection
Wellgate Pump
P M Clarke & J Maland
Double Wedding P M Clarke & F I Clarke
No16 Tram 1929
E L Scrivens Wellgate Early 1930's
Albion Road 1912
The Three Tuns 1905

Paul Nicholson & Clare Watts
Nicholsons Car Showroom x 2,
Wellgate House

Barbara Littlewood [Mr Mosses, Mr Tandy]
Wellgate Tunnel x 4 1978

Margaret Wilson
Private Schools x 4

Dr G B Peckitt
Ward, Rotherham Hospital Doncaster Gate
Nurse Jane Peckitt [nee Gillan]
Cartoon of Mr Anderson & Dr Sutherland

Philip H J Smedley
Wellgate School Demolition x 3
Wellgate Old Hall x 2
1 Wellgate Terrace,
81 Wellgate
Wellgate Junction, Mansfield Road
Behind 81 Wellgate
Mansfield Road & The Barn x 7
Harrison Proctor
Doncaster Gate Hospital
Adams Blacksmith x 2

C C Souter
Dedication Booklet,
St Georges Hall 1928

Donald Hodgkinson
Gerard Road Methodist Church x 4
Rotherham Advertiser Whit Walk

J S Crowther
Crowthers Stores 1903
Joseph Crowther

D Clover, P Thackray
E & A Clover Fishmongers 1926

John Hargreaves
The Barn
Kimbers Ephemera

David & John Clennell
Clifton Bank
81-81A Wellgate
Postcard Bromley Sands

Carol Smout
A Russell – Daily Independent 1936

Carol Burton
Frank Stockdale outside his shop 1935

Maureen & Roger Longdin
178 Wellgate

Child of Albany Street - Anonymous

D Wainman
Corner of Sherwood Crescent x 2

Joan & Philip Graham
1st World War Nursing Staff & patients
Rotherham Hospital Doncaster Gate x 4

Diane Shaw
Fred Elliott 1940
Rolls Royce 1945

M A Croft
Rotherham Dispensary Bottle
Brass Plaque
Phial

Paul & Janette Haigh
The Wishing Well x 6

Mrs W Mapplebeck
Receipt Rotherham Hospital